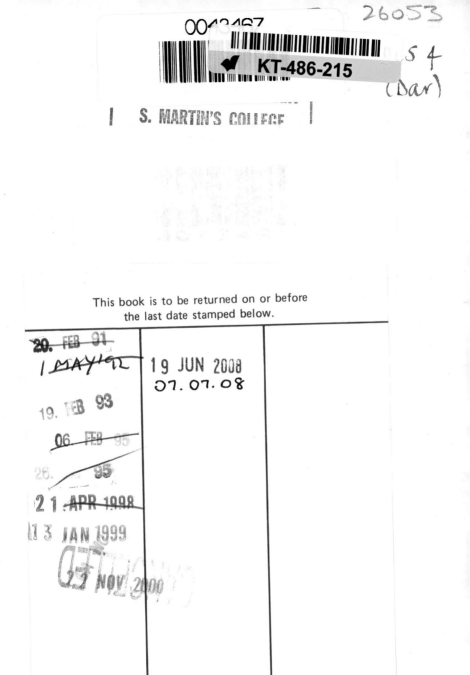

This book is to be returned on or before
the last date stamped below.

Fund-raising and Grant-aid

A practical and legal guide for charities and voluntary organisations

ANN DARNBROUGH AND DEREK KINRADE

WOODHEAD-FAULKNER · CAMBRIDGE

Published by Woodhead-Faulkner Limited
8 Market Passage, Cambridge CB2 3PF

First published 1980

© Ann Darnbrough and Derek Kinrade 1980

ISBN 0 85941 075 7

Whilst every effort has been made to ensure the accuracy of the
information in this book at the time of going to press, it is intended to
provide general guidance and should not be taken as a complete and
authoritative statement of the law.

Phototypesetting by County Set, Rayleigh, Essex
Printed in Great Britain by Biddles of Guildford

Contents

3

CONTENTS

Preface

Wisdom denotes the pursuing of the best ends by the best means
Francis Hutcheson (1694 – 1746)

Fund-raising is the backbone of the voluntary movement. Without it the vast range of services and institutions which so enrich the quality of our lives could never have been established, and the whole fabric of our society would be immeasurably poorer. It is impossible to estimate just what we would now be missing if voluntary funds and voluntary effort had not been forthcoming for the many thousands of projects which we so often take for granted.

Many of the services now provided statutorily and financed out of taxation originated through the generosity of the public and voluntary philanthropic endeavour. Voluntary enterprise is primarily concerned with the quality of life, whether establishing a local club or providing holidays at the seaside for disadvantaged children. Although the state increasingly takes responsibility in attempting to provide basic necessities, there will always remain a major role for the voluntary sector to fulfil wider needs and aspirations.

Of necessity, fund-raising must be commercially minded, but when stimulated and sustained by the needs of a good cause it can be a truly dedicated undertaking. We feel strongly that fund-raisers, however 'professional' they may be in their approach, should nevertheless remain firmly rooted in the cause for which they are working. It is our belief that while there may be quick profits in slick fund-raising techniques, the general public is not fooled in the long term, whereas it will always remain faithful to sincere calls upon its generosity.

Raising money, however, is not simply a matter of enthusiasm and running 'special events': the right approach is one which is appropriate both to the needs of the organisation and to the resources available to it, and this calls for knowledge and business acumen in those who shape policy, and a high degree of skill in those who organise the actual fund-raising. Our primary aim in writing this guide is to illuminate the aspects of the subject that call

5

for specialist knowledge and expertise, to throw light upon the legal undergrowth which threatens to trip up the unwary fund-raiser, and to face up to, chart and explain the obstacles (and opportunities) presented by our complex tax system.

Our own practical experience of fund-raising is rooted in the charitable sector and this is reflected throughout this guide. We are convinced that charitable fund-raising should seek to achieve two purposes: the obvious one of providing financial support for the benefiting organisation, the other to involve greater numbers of people in a wider understanding of the aims of the cause.

Nor is this all, for one cannot discuss fund-raising in the charitable sector without considering a number of overriding ethical considerations. In the first place, the acid test by which fund-raising should be evaluated is not how efficiently money is raised but how effectively it is spent. Nothing will dishearten fund-raisers and public faster than an organisation which is profligate or misguided in its use of donations. Hardly less important is the need to ensure that the expenses of fund-raising are kept within reasonable bounds. This is a difficult area, for it is certainly true that it is necessary to spend money to make money. When making direct appeals, expensive advertising and publicity may be justified in terms of a substantially enhanced return. Similarly, where fund-raising relies on a profit, the ratio of that profit to turnover, as in ordinary business, may be relatively low yet provide a satisfactory result overall. It is a matter of striking the right balance; of making sure that the financial end justifies the financial means, and can be seen to do so.

Charities are very much in the public eye and are particularly open to criticism. They need to be aware that they must consistently project a good image, in their fund-raising as much as in their general activities. One danger is that there are always people who are ready to use the good name of a charity to further their own interests, and liaisons with organisations and individuals who are not truly committed and involved in charitable works must always be viewed with caution and reserve. Equally, a reputable, caring charity should be careful not to involve itself in activities which tend to damage its reputation. It is very important that a responsible charity should at all times have in mind the purpose of its existence and that that purpose should be evident in everything it does. Credibility and consistency count for so much. Oxfam seems to us a model in this respect. It is not only highly skilled and successful in attracting funds, but is always mindful of its primary purposes: in the long term, a more just distribution of the world's resources and, in the shorter term, the alleviation of hunger and poverty. Thus its fund-raising programmes always have an educational aspect, and when appeals are made for financial support no opportunity is ever lost to project Oxfam's message.

Conversely, what are we to think of a charity which cares for children, but whose thrift shops are forlorn, dismal and dirty? Or of a charity for disabled people which campaigns for better access for its members, but arranges functions in places which present virtually insurmountable obstacles to a wheelchair?

Not all fund-raising is for charitable causes, however, and we have been careful not to forget other organisations – sporting and social clubs, dramatic societies, and other non-profit-making bodies – which also need funds. They will find many useful ideas as well as hard facts which they need to know. The sections on gaming and on government support for sport and the arts will be of particular interest to such groups.

We can guide our readers only a part of the way. Fund-raising is not merely a matter of knowledge and expertise: it also requires genuine talent. It is as much an art as a science, and demands qualities of flair, self-confidence, inventiveness and, above all, motivation which cannot be taught. Thus equipped, we see no limit to what may be achieved: the public will always respond to imaginative, original and genuine calls upon its goodwill.

Ann Darnbrough and Derek Kinrade

Acknowledgements

We should like to thank all those who have helped us to compile this guide: the public servants (who must remain nameless) who have assisted us in unravelling some of the deeper mysteries of the law and knotty problems in the tax system and who have checked our preliminary drafts; also Lily McToldridge, who did so much to produce our *Directory for the Disabled* and who has again been an incomparable support in the preparation of this manuscript. Finally, we must thank each other, for it is quite certain that neither one of us could have written this book alone.

1. Flag days

Given that the cause is one which elicits public sympathy, and also given fair weather, flag days can be a profitable and rewarding source of finance. There are a number of golden rules which must be observed to ensure success.

Locations

Concentrate on places where intense public activity provides the maximum opportunity for selling – markets, shopping centres, the precincts of bus and railway stations.

A word of caution on football grounds and other sports stadia, which attract large crowds: try to get permission to collect *inside* the ground and make the collection before the event and/or during an interval. People leaving are in too much of a hurry to get home to be sympathetic to a flagseller.

Personnel

A successful flag day requires an organiser with some administrative ability and a wealth of enthusiasm. The organiser's tasks are to choose the collecting centres, to gather together a sufficient team of helpers, to ensure that the law is observed and necessary authorisations are obtained, and to issue collecting tins etc. and publicity material and make sure that they are returned. Planning should begin some months in advance.

It is a mistake in a collection of any scale for one organiser to undertake the whole task of recruitment. Far better to search out and appoint suitable assistant organisers to take charge of each collecting centre. They will be better able to attract help among their own friends, neighbours and workmates who can then work as a team. Many methods of seeking help suggest themselves, but by far the most effective is personal contact, asking the potential collector outright, face to face, to collect on the appropriate day, even for only an hour. It may be that one can have too many collectors at one location, but we doubt it. Collectors are part of a team and not in rivalry, and the greater their number, the more likely it will be that the public will respond. What is really important is that as far as possible during all the busy hours of the day the collecting point is manned. A location which is covered for only half the day cannot be expected to yield anything like its full potential. If there are ten collectors available, it is far better that they work in shifts than, say, all on duty during the morning and none in the afternoon.

Publicity

Every opportunity should be taken to advertise the flag day in advance – local press and radio will normally help if properly approached. Posters should be displayed as widely as possible. More important, however, is that collectors are provided with the material to identify themselves and the cause for which they are collecting as boldly as possible.

On the whole, the general public is generously disposed to good causes, but people need to see without difficulty what it is they are being asked to support and to be satisfied that they are giving to a bona-fide collector. Someone hurrying about shopping needs to register the flagseller's presence and purpose at some distance so that there is time to stop and bring out the money. For these reasons, the collectors should display their authorisations; collecting tins and trays should be clearly labelled; and a promotional display should be provided. The promotional display must not, of course, obstruct the pavement, but it is usually possible to make a good show without getting in the way. A simple form of advertisement is a sandwich board with a poster on each side. This will stand on the ground or can even be worn.

It is a good idea to have at each collecting centre a table, perhaps in the forecourt of a shop (the shop may provide one), where a volunteer can sit to dispense spare tins, flags and publicity material and relieve collectors of full and heavy tins.

The law requires that the collector shall remain static and must not obstruct, annoy or 'importune' so as to harass any member of the public. Having said this, we think that there are dynamic attitudes to collecting, ways of projecting a positive personality and of calling attention to oneself which are perfectly legitimate. The shrinking violet who hides more in hope than expectation is unlikely to attract benevolence.

Documentation

Paperwork should be as simple as possible. The basic details of the collection can be recorded on a form like the one in Figure 1.1.

FLAG DAY COLLECTION				
Organisation _____ Collecting Centre _____				
Centre Organiser _____ Date _____				
Collector's name, address and telephone number	Authority number	No. of tins	Amount	Remarks

Figure 1.1 Specimen form for identifying street collectors and recording receipts

Each centre organiser should be issued with a form in duplicate well in advance of the flag day. The centre organiser then fills in columns 1 and 3 and returns the top copy in sufficient time to allow the issue of authorities and collecting materials. The authorities should be given a prefix identifying the charity and be numbered in blocks of one hundred for each collecting centre. After the collection, the amounts collected can be entered on the forms which can then be used to back up the account required by the licensing authority.

It is a good idea for the main organiser to keep a loose-leaf register of collectors which can be regularly up-dated with notes of when each volunteer turned out (see Figure 1.2).

Centre organisers, especially new ones, can then be provided with a photocopy when they get their record forms.

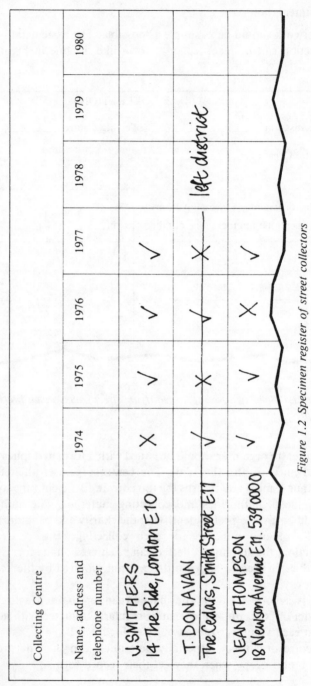

Collecting Centre	1974	1975	1976	1977	1978	1979	1980
Name, address and telephone number							
J. SMITHERS 14 The Ride, London E10	X	✓	✓	✓			
T. DONAVAN The Cedars, Smith Street E11	✓	X	✓	X —	left district		
JEAN THOMPSON 18 Newson Avenue E11. 539 0000	✓	✓	X	✓			

Figure 1.2 Specimen register of street collectors

No.

(name of organisation)

This is to certify that _____
(name and address of collector)

of _____
is authorised to collect on
behalf of _____ *(name of organisation)* _____

at _____

on _____ 19 ___
(no person under the age of 16 years may collect)

_____Organiser

_____ Address

Figure 1.3 Specimen authority card for street collectors

_____FLAG DAY _____ *(date)* _____

The contents of this box No. ──
will be collected by or may be returned to

_____

(name and address of centre organiser)

Please leave the seal intact

(name of organisation)

_____

_____

Figure 1.4 Specimen label for collecting tins

13

Law

England and Wales

Police, Factories etc. (Miscellaneous Provisions) Act 1916, s.5 and regulations made thereunder (as amended by the Local Government Act 1972, sch. 29, para. 22).

Scotland

Police, Factories etc. (Miscellaneous Provisions) Act 1916 as read with s.202 of the Local Government (Scotland) Act 1973.

Licensing authorities

Applications for permits to hold a street collection should be addressed to the relevant licensing authority, see page 23.

Licensing authorities usually adopt the following set of model regulations drawn up by the Home Office in 1974, and the model form of statement shown in Figure 1.5. There may be minor local variations. The Metropolitan Police use a different set of regulations, copies of which will be supplied by them on request.

Model street collection regulations

1. In these Regulations, unless the context otherwise requires:

'collection' means a collection of money or a sale of articles for the benefit of charitable or other purposes and the word 'collector' shall be construed accordingly;

'promoter' means a person who causes others to act as collectors;

'permit' means a permit for a collection;

'contributor' means a person who contributes to a collection and includes a purchaser of articles for sale for the benefit of charitable or other purposes;

'collecting box' means a box or other receptacle for the reception of money from contributors.

2. No collection, other than a collection taken at a meeting in the open air, shall be made in any street or public place within (the licensing authority's area) unless a promoter shall have obtained from the licensing authority a permit.

3. Application for a permit shall be made in writing not later than one month before the date on which it is proposed to make the collection:

Provided that the licensing authority may reduce the period of one month if satisfied that there are special reasons for so doing.

4. No collection shall be made except upon the day and between the hours stated in the permit.

Name of the person to whom the permit was granted: ....
Address of the person to whom the permit was granted: ....
....
Name of the charity or fund which is to benefit: ....
....
Date of collection:...

Show nil entries

Proceeds of collection	Amount	Total	Expenses and Application of Proceeds	Amount	Total
From collecting boxes			Printing & Stationery		
			Postage		
			Advertising		
Interest on proceeds			Collecting boxes		
			Badges		
Other items:			Emblems		
....			Other items:		
....			....		
			....		
			Payments approved under Regulation 15(2)		
			Disposal of Balance (insert particulars)		
TOTAL £			TOTAL £		

Certificate of the person to whom the permit was granted

I certify that to the best of my knowledge and belief the above is a true account of the proceeds, expenses and application of the proceeds of the collection.

Date .... (Signed) ....

Certificate of Accountant

I certify that I have obtained all the information and explanations required by me and that the above is in my opinion a true account of the proceeds, expenses and application of the proceeds of the collection.

Date .... (Signed) ....

Qualifications ....

Figure 1.5 Model form of statement for street collections

5. The licensing authority may, in granting a permit, limit the collection to such streets or public places or such parts thereof as it thinks fit.

6.—(1) No person may assist or take part in any collection without the written authority of a promoter.

(2) Any person authorised under paragraph (1) above shall produce such written authority forthwith for inspection on being requested to do so by a duly authorised officer of the licensing authority or any constable.

7. No collection shall be made in any part of the carriage way of any street which has a footway:

Provided that the licensing authority may, if it thinks fit, allow a collection to take place on the said carriage way where such collection has been authorised to be held in connection with a procession.

8. No collection shall be made in a manner likely to inconvenience or annoy any person.

9. No collector shall importune any person to the annoyance of such person.

10. While collecting:

    (a) a collector shall remain stationary; and

    (b) a collector or two collectors together shall not be nearer to another collector than 25 metres:

Provided that the licensing authority may, if it thinks fit, waive the requirements of this Regulation in respect of a collection which has been authorised to be held in connection with a procession.

11. No promoter, collector or person who is otherwise connected with a collection shall permit a person under the age of 16 years to act as a collector.

12.—(1) Every collector shall carry a collecting box.

(2) All collecting boxes shall be numbered consecutively and shall be securely closed and sealed in such a way as to prevent them being opened without the seal being broken.

(3) All money received by a collector from contributors shall immediately be placed in a collecting box.

(4) Every collector shall deliver, unopened, all collecting boxes in his possession to a promoter.

13. A collector shall not carry or use any collecting box, receptacle or tray which does not bear displayed prominently thereon the name of the charity or fund which is to benefit nor any collecting box which is not duly numbered.

14.—(1) Subject to paragraph (2) below a collecting box shall be opened in the presence of a promoter and another responsible person.

(2) Where a collecting box is delivered, unopened, to a bank, it may be opened by an official of the bank.

(3) As soon as a collecting box has been opened, the person opening it shall count the contents and shall enter the amount with the number of the collecting box on a list which shall be certified by that person.

15.—(1) No payment shall be made to any collector.

(2) No payment shall be made out of the proceeds of a collection, either directly or indirectly, to any other person connected with the promotion or conduct of such collection for, or in respect of, services connected therewith, except such payments as may have been approved by the licensing authority.

16.—(1) Within one month after the date of any collection the person to whom a permit has been granted shall forward to the licensing authority:

(a) a statement in the form set out in the Schedule to these Regulations, or in a form to the like effect, showing the amount received and the expenses and payments incurred in connection with such collection, and certified by that person and a qualified accountant;

(b) a list of the collectors;

(c) a list of the amounts contained in each collecting box;

and shall, if required by the licensing authority, satisfy it as to the proper application of the proceeds of the collection.

(2) The said person shall also, within the same period, at the expense of that person and after a qualified accountant has given his certificate under paragraph (1)(a) above, publish in such newspaper or newspapers as the licensing authority may direct a statement showing the name of the person to whom the permit has been granted, the area to which the permit relates, the name of the charity or fund to benefit, the date of the collection the amount collected, and the amount of the expenses and payments incurred in connection with such collection.

(3) The licensing authority may, if satisfied there are special reasons for so doing extend the period of one month referred to in paragraph (1) above.

(4) For the purposes of this Regulation 'a qualified accountant' means a member of one or more of the following bodies:

the Institute of Chartered Accountants in England and Wales;

the Institute of Chartered Accountants of Scotland;

the Association of Certified Accountants;

the Institute of Chartered Accountants in Ireland.

17. These regulations shall not apply:

(a) in respect of a collection taken at a meeting in the open air; or
(b) to the selling of articles in any street or public place when the articles are sold in the ordinary course of trade.

18. Any person who acts in contravention of any of the foregoing regulations shall be liable on summary conviction to a fine not exceeding £25 (as amended by Criminal Law Act 1977, Section 31).

2. House-to-house collections

House-to-house collecting is by no means unusual in Britain and is accepted as a legitimate and reasonable system of fund-raising. Most people respond generously and the occasional rebuff must be accepted philosophically. Whereas with flag days the receipts do not increase in proportion to the number of collectors (two people may take nearly as much as five), the results to be obtained from house-to-house collecting are directly proportional to the number of collectors recruited and it is on this primary base that the success of the collection must rest.

Recruitment of collectors

As with flag days, this is best achieved by the appointment of assistant organisers to be responsible for a given geographical area. Suitable districts can be marked off on a map, or, alternatively, one can divide up a voters' list. The more assistant organisers the better: not only will they help to share the burden of organisation but they will be able through personal knowledge to recruit their own teams, thus expanding the collecting force.

It cannot be repeated too often that the best method of recruitment is through personal contact – the direct, straightforward request – but other methods will suggest themselves: churches, voluntary organisations and social clubs can be approached. Appeals through press and radio can be tried; they may not yield dramatic results in terms of numbers but even one or two enthusiastic volunteers will help the cause, and the support thus attracted may prove to be valuable in other ways. House-to-house collecting is not a popular task and collectors are not easily won – *start early*.

Locations

Having divided up the territory to be covered into suitable districts, allocate individual streets to collectors as their time allows.

It is particularly important that area organisers ensure that two collectors are not allocated the same ground, and equally vital that no collector operates outside the alloted district unless special arrangements are agreed with the relevant area organiser. On receipt of the record forms the chief organiser should make a final check to see that no duplication of effort occurs. If, as is likely, it is not possible to recruit sufficient collectors to cover the whole territory, it is wise to take a hard-headed look at the allocation of available resources: the fact has to be faced that people in certain areas are more munificent than others, and one's efforts are best directed where the money is most forthcoming.

Timing

To be successful, a date should be chosen to avoid as far as possible summer holidays and yet allow as much evening collecting as possible. May and June are probably the best months. Many people are out during the day, and collecting is therefore best attempted in the early evening until darkness falls. It is unwise to continue after dark: residents are naturally suspicious and may be hostile to a collector who arrives on the doorstep at a late hour. This means that only a few hours collecting are possible on any day and that the task may have to be spread over two or more evenings, depending on the time available and the enthusiasm of the collector. Therefore, the longer the period of the collection the better – this can only spur the collectors to greater efforts. A fortnight seems to us a reasonable period if the necessary permission can be obtained.

Envelopes or tins?

Collectors have individual preferences and certainly choose between the two methods of collection. Envelopes require two visits against only one when using a collecting tin, but the delivery of the envelopes can be entrusted to a youngster, and our experience shows quite clearly that the yield from envelopes may be as much as double that obtained in tins in the same district. People have time to consider the merits of the cause, and to make a thoughtful contribution, rather than hurriedly delving for small change in front of the collector while he waits at the door. The envelope can be passed round the family and be ready for the collector's knock, saving a great deal of time. Some people, of course, lose the envelope or reckon that it has been eaten by the dog, but the sharp collector carries spares and loses no more time than if he had proffered a tin.

Method of approach

Householders are rightly suspicious when a stranger appears on the doorstep. They need to be reassured. The collector should, in the first place, present a good appearance. He should wear his badge prominently, and should state the purpose of his visit clearly and politely. A friendly approach goes a long way to breaking down barriers, and establishing the genuineness of the collection. All this is fairly obvious, but it is surprising how often the approach is vague and ambiguous. A shadowy figure appears at your door and mutters, 'I'm collecting up the envelopes for the MS', or some such phrase. A preliminary friendly greeting is not only a friendly sign, it gives the potential donor a moment or two to collect himself, to weigh you up and to prepare himself for your message.

Documentation

The basic form is similar to that for flag days (Chapter 1). A form is required for issue in duplicate to each area organiser to record details of the collectors, streets allocated, and the number of envelopes or tins required (see Figure 2.1).

The top copy should be returned to the chief organiser in plenty of time for him to check for duplicated allocations, and to issue the authorities, badges and collecting materials. It is recommended that the authorities be given a distinctive prefix and that they be numbered in blocks of one hundred for each district (avoiding confusion with any concurrent collection). After the collection, the amounts collected can be filled in and the forms used to back up the account required by the licensing authority.

It is useful for the chief organiser to keep a loose-leaf register of collectors district by district which can be regularly updated and used to note collections year by year (see Figure 1.2 for a suggested format). Area organisers can then be provided in the following year with a photocopy to identify potential collectors in that district.

Law

The relevant law is contained in the House-to-House Collections Act 1939, amended by the Local Government Act 1972 and the Local Government (Scotland) Act 1973. Note that 'house' includes a place of business and that this act does not apply to collectors operating with a licence issued under the Pools Competitions Act 1971.

Regulations have been made under the Act. For England they are

HOUSE-TO-HOUSE COLLECTION

Organisation _____ Area _____

Area Organiser _____ Dates _____

Collector's name, address and telephone number	Authority no.	Streets, etc., covered	No. of tins or envelopes	Amount

Figure 2.1 Specimen form for identifying house-to-house collectors and recording receipts

the House-to-House Collections Regulations 1947, amended by the House-to-House Collections Regulations 1963. For Scotland they are the House-to-House Collections (Scotland) Regulations 1948.

The law can be summarised as follows:

1. The collection must be for 'charitable purposes'.
2. The collection must be *licensed*, and to promote a collection or to collect without a licence is an offence. The only exceptions to this are:
   (*a*) Collections which are purely 'local in character'. These may be authorised by *certificate* issued by the relevant authority.
   (*b*) National charities that wish to promote collections over a wide area may be authorised by *exemption order* made by the Home Secretary. In practice, this is restricted to collections involving about 70 or more widely dispersed localities.
3. Applications for licence, when one is required, must be made by the promoter of the collection to the relevant authority, as follows:
   (*a*) In the Metropolitan Police District: a *single* application to the Metropolitan Commissioner of Police to embrace all relevant localities.
   (*b*) In the City of London: to the Common Council.
   (*c*) Elsewhere in England and Wales: individual applications to the district council for the localities in which the collection will take place.
   (*d*) In Scotland: an islands or district council.
4. Applications for licences or exemption orders must be made at least one month before the first day of the month in which the collection is to be held (e.g. on or before 1 August for 16 September) but belated applications can be allowed in special circumstances. The wording of the application is shown in the regulations, but in practice forms can be obtained from the relevant authority.
5. Licences normally cover any period up to 12 months (in certain circumstances, up to 18 months) depending on the terms of the application or the administrative practice of the authority.
6. The authority must be satisfied, *inter alia*, that the proportion of the proceeds applied to charitable purposes is adequate (i.e. that 'expenses' are not excessive), and that the promoter is 'a fit and proper person' who can be relied on to

ensure that the collectors are equally 'fit and proper persons', who will conduct the collection in accordance with the relevant law.

7. Provision is made for appeal against refusal to grant a licence except when acting under a certificate (see 2(*a*) above), which will set out the appropriate conditions.

8. To avoid overlapping, district councils are recommended to maintain a register to include all house-to-house collections, however authorised. Local organisers should, therefore, check that their intended collection dates are not in conflict with those of other charities and, when authorised, are duly recorded.

Promoters and collectors are required to comply with the following regulations, and contravention of them or failure to comply with them constitutes an offence (references to collecting by receipt books have been omitted).

Promoters must apply for licence or exemption order (see 4 above), and, if granted, must:

(*a*) 'Exercise all due diligence' to secure that collectors are 'fit and proper persons' and that they comply with the appropriate regulations.

(*b*) Issue an authority and badge (see Figures 2.2 and 2.3) obtained from Her Majesty's Stationary Office, to each collector completed as appropriate.

(*c*) Issue a collecting box indicating clearly the purpose of the collection. The box must be securely closed and sealed in such a way that it cannot be opened without breaking the seal, and must bear an identifying number; or issue envelopes (which must have gummed flaps).

(*d*) 'Exercise all due diligence' to secure that authorities, badges and collecting boxes are not issued to a collector before his name and address have been entered on a list, together with the identifying number of the collecting box(es), and that all are returned on completion of the collection (or when a collector for any other reason ceases to act as such).

(*e*) Examine all collecting boxes and envelopes and, if they contain money, open them in the presence of another responsible person. The contents shall be counted immediately and the amount entered on a list (in the case of boxes against the identifying number of the box) which must be certified by the persons making the examination.

(*f*) Furnish to the authority an account of the collection within

Front

HOUSE-TO-HOUSE COLLECTIONS ACT
COLLECTOR'S CERTIFICATE OF AUTHORITY

(Here insert name of collector in block letters)
of *(here insert address of collector)*
is hereby authorised to collect for
(here insert the purpose of the collection)
in *(here insert the area within which the collector is authorised to collect, being an area within which the collection has been authorised)*
*during the period *(here insert the period during which the collector is authorised to collect, being a period during which the collection has been authorised).*

Signature of collector   Signed†

*This entry may be omitted in the case of a collection in respect of which an exemption order has been made.
†The authority should be signed by or on behalf of the chief promoter of the collection (i.e. the person to whom the licence or exemption order was granted).

Back

Every collector shall:
(a) sign his name on the prescribed certificate of authority issued to him and produce it on the demand of any police constable or of any occupant of a house visited by him for the purpose of collection;
(b) sign his name on the prescribed badge issued to him and wear the badge prominently whenever he is engaged in collecting; and
(c) keep such certificate and badge in his possession and return them to a promoter of the collection on replacement thereof or when the collection is completed or at any other time on the demand of a promoter of the collection.

Figure 2.2 Form of prescribed certificate of authority for house-to-house collections

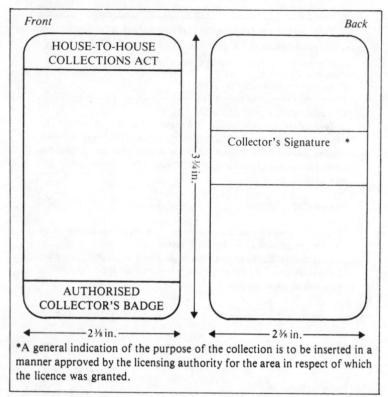

Front *Back*

HOUSE-TO-HOUSE
COLLECTIONS ACT

Collector's Signature *

AUTHORISED
COLLECTOR'S BADGE

3¾ in.

◄————— 2⅜ in. —————►   ◄————— 2⅜ in. —————►

*A general indication of the purpose of the collection is to be inserted in a manner approved by the licensing authority for the area in respect of which the licence was granted.

Figure 2.3 Form of prescribed badge for house-to-house collectors

one month of the expiry of the licence. If the collection took place under the authority of an exemption order the person to whom the order was granted must furnish the account to the Home Secretary annually, or within three months of the date of any revocation of the order (in special circumstances, extensions may be allowed). The account shall be in the form shown in Figure 2.4. The account shall be accompanied by vouchers for each item of expenses and application of the proceeds and by the lists referred to in paragraphs (*d*) and (*e*) above, unless the account is certified by an auditor who is a member of an association or society of accountants incorporated at 12 December 1947 or accepted as competent by the authority. (If vouchers and lists are not required to be submitted, they must nevertheless be retained for three months, and made available to the authority if required.)

(g) Ensure that all forms of certificates of authority and badges are destroyed when no longer required in connection with that collection or a further collection which he has been authorised to promote for the same purpose.

Surname of chief promoter (in block letters).
Other names (in block letters).
Address of chief promoter.
Purpose of collection.
Area to which account relates.
Periód to which account relates.

All amounts to be entered gross.

Proceeds of collection	£	p	Expenses and application of proceeds	£	p
From collectors, as in lists of collectors and amounts attached hereto.			Printing and stationery		
Bank interest			Postage		
Other items (if any)			Advertising		
			Collecting boxes		
			Other items (if any)		
			Disposal of Balance (insert particulars)		
Total			Total		

Certificate of chief promoter
I certify that to the best of my knowledge and belief the above is a true account of the expenses, proceeds and application of the proceeds of the collection to which it relates.
Date   Signed

Certificate of auditor
I certify that I have obtained all the information and explanations required by me as auditor and that the above is in my opinion a true account of the expenses, proceeds and application of the proceeds of the collection to which it relates.
Date   Signed
Qualifications

Figure 2.4 Form of prescribed account for house-to-house collections

Collectors:

(*a*) Shall comply with the regulations shown on the back of the certificate of authority (see Figure 2.2).

(*b*) Shall be aged at least 16 years (*18 years* in the Metropolitan Police District or the City of London).

(*c*) Shall not importune any person so as to cause him annoyance, nor remain in or at the door of any house if requested to leave by any of its occupants.

(*d*) When collecting by means of a collecting box, shall not receive any contribution except by permitting the contributor to place it in the box, and shall return the box with its seal unbroken to the promoter:

  (i) when the box is full, or

  (ii) if the promoter so requests, or

  (iii) if he decides not to act as a collector, or

  (iv) at the end of the collection.

(*e*) When collecting by means of envelopes, shall not receive any contribution except in an envelope which has been securely closed by the gummed flap, and shall return all envelopes (unopened if they contain contributions):

  (i) if the promoter so requests, or

  (ii) if he decides not to act as a collector, or

  (iii) at the end of the collection.

The telephone numbers of the relevant Civil Service Departments are 01-233 5404 (England) and 031-556 8400 (Scotland).

3. Lotteries

You don't have to be a genius to organise a lottery . . . but it helps! No, not really, but the whole subject is wrapped up in some pretty formidable law.

How they work

To start with, we must try to define what a lottery is. If you thought you knew, how about this:

> A distribution of prizes where the results are determined by chance factors outside the control of the participants, and each prizewinner is ascertained by reference to not more than three determining factors, each of which is either the result of a draw or other determination or the outcome of an event.

If you care to read that again, you will see that the heart of the matter is that the person taking part accepts a chance offered to him, say a numbered draw ticket, or makes some blind choice. Conversely, if the entrant exercises a deliberate choice or forecast then he is betting or gaming and is outside the provisions of the lottery law (and in a quite different and even more deadly legal minefield). Note that bingo falls outside the definition of a lottery.

We don't intend to belabour the various kinds of lotteries. These include draws, raffles, sweepstakes and tombola; the permutations on these themes are infinite and, fortunately, well known. We leave it to you to choose the kind of lottery best suited to your needs and resources, be it a raffle at a cheese and wine evening, a regular weekly draw, or a large-scale lottery. All share a common advantage of being a relatively popular way of raising funds. Lottery tickets of any kind are a good deal easier to sell than flagday emblems. They offer value for money: the chance to win an attractive prize for a small outlay, a prospect which appeals to a primitive instinct in many people.

But no one should imagine that running a lottery is an easy matter. It requires a lot of work and dedication if it is to succeed in achieving its full potential. This is particularly true of the weekly lottery: the spirit of the best organiser can wilt over hundreds of successive weeks, not to mention that of the contributors. If that kind of commitment is available, well and good, for 52 lots of proceeds each year can add up to a sizeable amount. Our experience suggests that such lotteries are best suited to organisations able to command an enthusiastic but only limited support. Those which enjoy a claim to wider public sympathy would do well to consider a larger-scale lottery, looking to the support of a much greater number of people on an occasional, perhaps annual, basis. The advantages are obvious. One can offer more substantial prizes and can utilise a large number of ticket sellers who are willing to help a good cause on an irregular basis. If the object is a deserving one, many commercial firms may be persuaded to donate the prizes and a great occasion can be made of the actual draw with a celebrity to perform the ceremony.

One practical point to watch is the price of the tickets and how they are made up into books. If tickets are offered cheaply at 4p or 5p each with five tickets in each book so that the value of each book works out to a simple round figure, then there is a very good chance that people will buy one or more whole books at a time, whereas if the tickets are expensive, they will tend to restrict their generosity. It is a simple matter of human psychology, depending of course on the value of the prizes one is able to offer. When approaching people to donate prizes it is important to present yourself and your cause well. Make the request in person or by a well written business-like letter, preferably typed, which makes clear the standing of your organisation and the worth of your purposes.

And now to the law. Don't be put off. The choice of the different styles of lottery recognised by law is fairly simple and straight-forward. Thereafter, it is just a question of following the rules.

Law

It is important to recognise that lotteries are *illegal* except as specifically allowed by the Lotteries and Amusements Act 1976.

The 1976 Act (which with the Lotteries Regulations 1977 and the Lotteries (Scotland) Regulations 1977 consolidates and extends previous legislation) permits several types of lotteries:

    (*a*) Local-authority lotteries
    (*b*) Societies' lotteries

(c) Small lotteries incidental to exempt entertainments

(d) Private lotteries

(e) Lotteries provided as 'amusements with prizes' at certain commercial entertainments.

The first and last of these are not relevant to charities but the others are and will now be discussed in detail.

Note that individual branches of a society may each regard themselves as 'a society' in reading the notes which follow. Provided that each fulfils the conditions and is separately registered there is nothing to preclude different branches holding concurrent lotteries even though in aggregate they exceed the specified limits.

Societies' lotteries

These are lotteries promoted on behalf of a society which is established and conducted wholly or mainly for one or more of the following purposes:

(a) charitable purposes;

(b) participation in or support of athletic sports or games or cultural activities;

(c) other purposes which are neither purposes of private gain nor purposes of any commercial undertaking.

This last general definition needs some amplification. A lottery is not illegal just because its proceeds (or part of them) end up in a particular individual's pocket, so long as that individual's gain is in fact part of the society's purpose and benefits the society as a whole.

This means that the whole or part of the proceeds could be applied to the needs of an individual member – say by buying a kidney machine for his exclusive use – without this being construed as 'private gain'. Professional help can legitimately be employed, provided that the limit placed on expenses is not exceeded. Organisations will hardly need to be advised, however, that great circumspection must be exercised in relation to proposals for fund-raising lotteries operated by commercial undertakings or by private individuals. The employment of an 'unsuitable person' could result in loss of the society's registration quite apart from the risk of legal proceedings arising from any misdemeanour by such a person acting on the society's behalf.

Professional, expert help can be an enormous spur to fund-raising, particularly in major schemes, but as we have remarked elsewhere it is essential to distinguish between help which assists and help which exploits.

31

The 1976 Act is silent on the matter of professional agents, but in their Report for 1977, the Gaming Board comment:

Providing their fees do not take the lottery expenses beyond the authorised limits, and provided also that there is no suggestion that responsibility for the lottery is removed from the local authority or society, it does not seem that there is any bar to the involvement of agents. The Board's information is that a number of lotteries are being run with the help of agents. On the other hand, a number of local authorities and societies seem to be managing very well without agents and, if anything, expenses overall show a tendency to be lower where they are not employed. However, direct comparisons are difficult and the Board do not seek to influence local authorities or societies in deciding whether or not to employ agents.

Later in the report, however, the Board do point out that, 'the risk of criminal involvement in lotteries is bound to arise and the prime safeguard must lie in the care with which local authorities and societies order their affairs.' We would, of course, echo this, but if the character of a professional agent is above reproach the question is really whether the probability of additional expenditure in fees will be offset through increased proceeds resulting from the agent's expertise and outlets. Our own warnings have been heavily under-lined in the 1978 report of the Royal Commission on Gambling which comments on an unacceptable degree of commercial exploitation.

The law now provides for two levels of societies' lotteries: those in which the value of tickets or chances sold is £5000 or less, and those where it exceeds £5000. The following conditions apply to both levels unless otherwise stated: where additional or different conditions apply to lotteries *over* £5000, these are indicated in *italic* type after the corresponding provision for lotteries under £5000.

1. The lottery must be promoted in Great Britain (i.e. the United Kingdom excluding Northern Ireland).

2. The promoting society must be registered under Schedule 1 to the Act (registration is explained below).

3. The lottery must be promoted in accordance with a scheme approved by the society. The scheme must specify:
   (a) The name and address of the society by which the scheme was approved.
   (b) The name and address of the registration authority.
   (c) The date of registration.
   (d) The reference number (if any) of the registration.

(e) The period during which it is to have effect. It must not have effect for a period of more than three years.

(f) In the case of a scheme having effect for less than 12 months, the number of lotteries which may be promoted under it. In any other case, the number of lotteries which may be promoted under it in any period of 12 months. In either case, the scheme must require that the number so specified shall not be exceeded.

(g) A proportion (not exceeding one half) as being the proportion of the whole proceeds of any lottery under the scheme which may be appropriated for the provision of prizes in that lottery. The scheme must require that the proportion so specified shall not be exceeded unless:

   (i) the proceeds of the lottery fall short of the sum reasonably estimated; and

   (ii) the appropriation is made to fulfil an unconditional undertaking about prizes given in connection with the sale of the relevant tickets or chances: and

   (iii) the total amount appropriated in respect of prizes does not exceed the amount which would have been appropriated out of the proceeds of the lottery if the proceeds had amounted to the sum reasonably estimated.

A copy of the scheme is submitted to the registration authority (see page 38).

Additionally, for lotteries over £5000, the scheme must specify both the amount or value of the largest or most valuable prize which may be offered and the total value of the tickets or chances which may be sold in:

(a) any short-term lottery under the scheme;

(b) any medium-term lottery under the scheme;

(c) any other lottery under the scheme.

(These terms are defined later.) The scheme must require that these sums shall not be exceeded. Societies may, if they wish, give details for all three options. Schemes for lotteries over £5000 must be registered with the Gaming Board before any tickets or chances are sold. The Gaming Board is at Africa House, 64/78 Kingsway, London WC2B 6BW. Applications have to be made on form GBL1 and there is a fee of £100. The Gaming Board has published a model scheme (see page 37) which represents the Board's minimum requirements. Any scheme may include additional provisions not required by the regulations.

4.   The total value of tickets or chances to be sold must not exceed £5000.
The total value of tickets or chances sold must not exceed:
for a short-term lottery: £10,000
for a medium-term lottery: £20,000
for any other lottery: £40,000

5. The whole proceeds of the lottery, after deducting sums lawfully appropriated on account of expenses (see 15 below) or for the provision of prizes (see 14 below) must be applied to the charitable purposes of the society.

6. No society shall hold more than 52 such lotteries in any period of 12 months, but when the dates of two or more societies' lotteries promoted on behalf of one society are the same and the total value of the tickets or chances to be sold in those lotteries does not exceed £10,000, all those lotteries shall be treated as one.

7. The date of any lottery promoted on behalf of a society shall be not less than seven days after the date of any previous lottery promoted on behalf of that society.

8. The promoter must be a member of the society and must be authorised in writing by the governing body to act as such (in the case of a lottery run by a branch, the governing body would normally be the branch committee, which would minute its authority).

9. Every ticket and every lawful notice or advertisement for the lottery must specify the name of the society, the name and address of the promoter, and the date of the lottery.

10. No ticket or chance may be sold for more than 25p.

11. The price of every ticket must be the same and each ticket must be marked with its price.

12. No one must be allowed to participate in the lottery in respect of a ticket or chance unless he has paid the whole price for it, and money received for a ticket must not be returned. (Offers of, say, five tickets for the price of four are not allowed.)

13. No prize shall exceed £1000 in amount or value ('value' may be construed as the normal market price of the prize on sale by retail).
No prize shall exceed the following sums:
for short-term lotteries: £1000
for medium-term lotteries: £1500
for other lotteries: £2000

14. The amount appropriated for the provision of prizes must not exceed one-half of the whole proceeds (i.e. the total value of tickets or chances sold).

15. The amount of the proceeds appropriated on account of expenses (exclusive of prizes) must not exceed whichever is the less of:
    (a) the expenses actually incurred, or

(b) 25 per cent of the whole proceeds.

The amount of the proceeds appropriated on account of expenses (exclusive of prizes) must not exceed whichever is the less of:

(a) the expenses actually incurred, or

(b) 15 per cent of the whole proceeds, or such larger percentage (not exceeding 25 per cent) as the Gaming Board may authorise in the case of a particular lottery.

The Gaming Board have indicated that where their authorisation is sought for expenses greater than 15 per cent of the proceeds (s. 11(13)(b) of the Act), the maximum levels of expenses which the Board would be likely to view sympathetically are generally as follows:

Proceeds of lottery	Maximum expenses likely to be authorised
£10,000	£2250
£15,000	£3000
£20,000	£3750
£25,000	£4250
£30,000	£4750
£35,000	£5250

It cannot, however, be assumed that these maxima will necessarily be authorised in particular cases. The Board advise that they will always be concerned to satisfy themselves that the expenses are the lowest compatible with the successful operation of each lottery.

16. The promoter must make a return in accordance with Schedule 1 to the Act, not later than the end of the third month after the date of the lottery, to the registration authority (see page 38). The return must be certified by two other members of the society, being persons of full age appointed in writing by the governing body of the society, showing:

(a) a copy of the scheme under which the lottery was promoted;

(b) the whole proceeds of the lottery;

(c) the sums appropriated out of those proceeds on account of expenses and prizes respectively;

(d) the purpose to which the balance of the proceeds was applied and the amount so applied;

(e) the date of the lottery.

The Gaming Board require in respect of each lottery promoted under a registered scheme a brief statement of account on form GBL 4. On occasion they will seek more detailed accounts. In respect of each registered scheme, if more than one lottery is held, a lottery fee is payable in respect of such lottery including the first as follows:

Total value of tickets of chances sold in the lottery	Fee
£5001 – £10,000	£15
over £10,000	£20

Such fees are additional to the scheme registration fee of £100.

17. No tickets or chances shall be sold by or to a person who has not attained the age of 16 years.

18. No tickets or chances shall be sold to a person in any street, except by a person present in a kiosk or shop premises having no space for the accommodation of customers (a 'street' includes any bridge, road, lane, footway, subway, court, alley or passage, whether a thoroughfare or not, which is for the time being open to the public without payment).

19. No ticket or chance shall be sold to a person:
    (*a*) In a licensed betting office.
    (*b*) In an amusement arcade.
    (*c*) In a bingo or gaming club.

20. No ticket or chance shall be sold by means of a vending machine.

21. No ticket or chance shall be sold by a person when visiting any other person at his home in the discharge of any official, professional or commercial function not connected with lotteries.

The 'date' of the lottery is defined as the date on which the winners in the lottery are ascertained. Where there is no 'draw' for this purpose (i.e. where the winners are ascertained by reference to what is printed on the tickets), the date will be regarded as the last day on which the tickets are on sale.

Although prizes and expenses are limited as stated in 14 and 15 above, it is possible that either or both will exceed the proportions allowed because they are the subject of an unconditional undertaking whereas the proceeds of the lottery fall short of what was reasonably expected. This situation is allowed for in 13(3) of the Act *as a defence against prosecution*. Plainly, however, it is a situation which should be avoided if possible. It is recommended that in planning a lottery the level of expenses and prizes should be kept below 25 and 50 per cent respectively of an estimate of proceeds which is the *lowest* that can reasonably be expected.

A *short-term lottery* is defined as one where less than one month has passed since the society's previous lottery.

A *medium-term lottery* is defined as one where less than three months but not less than one month has passed since the society's previous lottery.

'Other' lotteries are not defined, but may of course be regarded as those where three months or more has passed since the society's previous lottery.

The Act is silent on the subject of unclaimed prizes. It is known, however, that some societies and local authorities seek to keep down administrative expenses by keeping no record of the purchasers of tickets, leaving them to claim their prizes if successful when the winning numbers are announced. These arrangements create a very real risk that some prizes will be unclaimed. This raises serious legal issues of civil liabilities which must be solved by the courts not the Gaming Board. However, the Board does urge promoters to recognise in advance the difficulties which can result from unrecorded sales and to act on advice in determining the course they wish to follow (*Report of the Gaming Board for Great Britain 1977*, para. 118).

The Gaming Board's model scheme for a society's lottery over £5000

The scheme, details of which are given below, was approved on —— by the ——, a society established for the purpose of ——.

By this scheme, which shall have effect for not more than three years from the date on which it is registered by the Gaming Board for Great Britain, the above-mentioned society, which is for the time being registered in pursuance of Schedule 1 to the Lotteries and Amusements Act 1976 with —— (having become so registered on —— under reference number ——), indicate that they propose to promote not more than 52 lotteries, subject to the provisions of section 10(1)(a) of the Lotteries and Amusements Act 1976, in any 12-month period during the validity of the scheme.

When any two or more lotteries are to be held on behalf of the society on the same day, the total value of tickets sold in those lotteries shall not exceed £10,000 and any such lotteries have been counted as single lotteries in determining the total number of lotteries above.

There will be an interval of at least seven days between the dates of any lotteries promoted under the scheme, except where tickets are to be sold wholly or mainly to persons attending a particular sporting or athletic event. No medium-term lottery will be promoted less than one month after a previous lottery and no other lottery will be promoted less than three months after a previous lottery.

The total value of tickets to be sold in any lottery to be promoted under the scheme shall not exceed:
£10,000 for any short-term lottery.
£20,000 for any medium-term lottery.
£40,000 for any other lottery.

The amount or value of the single largest prize to be awarded in any lottery to be promoted under the scheme shall not exceed:
£1000 for any short-term lottery.

£1500 for any medium-term lottery.

£2000 for any other lottery.

and the proportion of the whole proceeds of any lottery which may be appropriated for prizes in that lottery shall not exceed 50 per cent except in the special circumstances mentioned in section 13(3) of the Lotteries and Amusements Act 1976.

It is expected that the total number of each type of lottery to be promoted during the validity of the scheme will not exceed:

—— short-term

—— medium-term

—— other lotteries

Registration of societies' lotteries (whether under or over £5000)

Registration must be effected under the Lotteries and Amusements Act 1976, Sch. 1. Application must be made to the relevant local authority for the address of the society. In England this is the London borough council, or the district council, or the Common Council of the City of London, or the Council of the Isles of Scilly; in Wales, it is the district council; in Scotland, it is the islands or district council. The application is to specify the purposes for which the society is established and conducted. An initial registration fee of £10 is chargeable. This is renewable on 1 January in each year of registration at a fee of £5. (Prior registration under Sch. 7 to the Betting, Gaming and Lotteries Act 1963 counts as registration under the 1976 Act.)

Small lotteries incidental to exempt entertainments

Typical examples are lotteries held at bazaars, fêtes, dances, etc.

The whole proceeds of the entertainment *and* lottery, except for permitted deductions, must be devoted to purposes other than private gain (see pages 31 and 44). The permitted deductions are:

1. The expenses of the entertainment (but not those of the lottery).
2. The expenses of printing the lottery tickets.
3. The cost of prizes up to £50, or such greater sum as may be specified by order of the Secretary of State (by statutory instrument).

The prizes must not be of money.

Tickets or chances in the lottery may be sold or issued and the result announced only at the place of and during the entertainment.

The facilities for participating in the lottery (together with any other facilities for participating in lotteries or gaming) shall not be the only, or the only substantial, inducement to persons to attend the entertainment.

Private lotteries

This category includes, *inter alia*, lotteries in Great Britain which are promoted for, and in which the sale of tickets or chances is confined to, members of one society established and conducted for purposes not connected with gaming, betting or lotteries (local branches being regarded as separate and distinct 'societies' for this purpose).

The promoters must be society members and authorised in writing by the governing body of the society (normally the branch committee) to promote the lottery.

The whole proceeds, except the cost of printing and stationery, must be devoted either to providing prizes, or to the purposes of the society, or to both.

Written notice or advertisement must be confined to the tickets and the premises of the benefiting society.

The price of every ticket or chance must be the same, and be stated on the ticket, together with (on the face) the names and addresses of the promoters, a statement of the persons to whom the sale of tickets is restricted (i.e. the members of the society) and a further statement that no prize will be paid or delivered to anyone other than the person to whom the winning ticket was sold. (This statement must, of course, be observed in practice.)

No ticket or chance may be issued except by way of sale, and for the full stated price; no sale money may be returned.

Tickets must not be sent by post.

The future of lotteries

The potential of lotteries is enormous. In Spain, for example, the state-run lottery, 'El Gordo', offers a total of 254,000 prizes representing over £150 million and including 25 first prizes of £1,300,000 each! The lottery grosses over £200 million and after deduction of prize money and expenses contributes more than £40 million to charities and sport. In Britain, after a slow start following the introduction of the 1976 Act, there has been a steady increase in the number of societies and local authorities seeking registration with the Gaming Board to promote the larger-scale lotteries. By the end of 1977, 149 local authorities and 162 societies had registered schemes and by April 1978 the total number of schemes had jumped to 642. In their annual report for 1977, the

Gaming Board commented: 'Saturation point for the market in lottery tickets must lie somewhere ahead, and sooner or later new registrations may be expected to tail off, but there is no present indication that this point is near.'

The Royal Commission on Gambling, reporting in July 1978, was strongly in favour of a national lottery for good causes run by a national lottery board.

4. Bingo

The appeal

As a game, bingo neither demands skill nor provides intellectual stimulation. Rather, it owes its phenomenal popularity to the communal social spirit which its devotees enjoy (and which commercial promoters are at pains to encourage) combined with the thrill of competing with other players in a series of races towards attractive prizes. In the post-war years bingo has proved to be one of the most lucrative growth industries, and though the level of interest has now reached a plateau, it shows no sign of imminent collapse. Astute fund-raisers cannot ignore the potential of so popular a pastime.

In particular, the arrangements set out on page 43 provide a limited opportunity within the specified conditions both to raise money and to utilise premises which might otherwise be put to no good use. Societies should not be discouraged from the promotion of such bingo games because they have no obvious person in their ranks to arrange and conduct the sessions. The organisation of a game such as bingo may well appeal to someone who is not otherwise attracted by the normal work of the society which may be of a dull 'committee' nature or call for a high social commitment. Moreover, in attracting players to bingo games, the society may well be attracting people who can help them in other ways and who may offer their services without any coercion as a result of the contact established.

The game of bingo appears in many forms, but the basic principle of all is that each player receives a 'card' listing a distinctive set of numbers. A 'caller' selects and calls numbers at random, which the players cancel from their 'cards'. The first player to delete all the required numbers in any one specified game – e.g. top, middle or bottom line; a pyramid; or all the numbers on his card – is the winner. There are many variations in the way in which the cards can be utilised, and many ways of achieving a random selection of the numbers. These are well known and need no elaboration here.

What is of vital concern is that local organisations operate within the provisions of the law. We make the assumption that societies, clubs and charities wishing to raise funds to further their own activities or simply to provide bingo as an amusement will wish to operate on a basis which avoids altogether the necessity for licensing or registration and excise duty. The relevant conditions under which this happy exception may be achieved are set out in the Gaming Act 1968, the Betting and Gaming Duties Act 1972 and the Lotteries and Amusements Act 1976.

Conditions for exemption from licensing or registration and from payment of duty

It is important to appreciate that bingo is a form of gaming and that apart from the specific exceptions which follow, persons and clubs promoting bingo must be either licensed or registered under the social law and must pay bingo duty under the revenue law.

None of the following exceptions can be used by clubs licensed or registered under the Gaming Act 1968.

Bingo played as a small-scale amusement at a club

The club must be constituted and conducted in good faith as a club and must have at least 25 members; it must be so constituted and conducted, in respect of membership and otherwise, as not to be of a temporary character (Gaming Act 1968, s.40).

No levy may be charged on the stakes or the winnings, i.e. all stake money must be returned as prizes (Gaming Act 1968, s.4).

The subscription for membership must not exceed £3 a year (Betting and Gaming Duties Act 1972, Sch. 3, para. 2). This need not be paid all at once, but instalments must not be more frequent than quarterly (Gaming Act 1968, s.3).

Apart from the membership subscription, entry to the place where bingo is played must cost not more than 10p (Betting and Gaming Duties Act 1972, Sch. 3, para. 2) for the whole day (Gaming Act 1968, s.3, s.40).

No other payment (e.g. a participation fee) may be charged and no obligation to make any other payment may be required to be incurred, in order to enable a person to play bingo (Betting and Gaming Duties Act 1972, Sch. 3, para. 2). Stake money is not regarded as another payment and there is, in fact, no restriction on stakes.

The public may not be admitted (Gaming Act 1968, s.5).

Bingo provided by societies as an amusement at non-commercial entertainments

This exemption applies to bazaars, sales of work, fêtes, dinners, dances, sporting and athletic events, and similar entertainments whether limited to one day or extending over two or more days (Lotteries and Amusements Act 1976, s.3(1)).* For the meaning of 'society' see page 44.

The whole proceeds of the entertainment apart from legitimate expenses (including expenses incurred in connection with the provision of bingo and prizes) must be devoted to purposes other than private gain (Lotteries and Amusements Act 1976, s.15(4)).* For the meaning of 'private gain' see pages 31 and 44.

The facilities for winning bingo prizes, with or without any other facilities offered for taking part in lotteries or gaming, must not be the only, or the only substantial inducement to persons to attend the entertainment (Lotteries and Amusements Act 1976, s.15(4)).*

Bingo played at entertainments promoted by societies to raise money for purposes other than private gain

The rules covering this are in s. 41 of the Gaming Act 1968 and para. 4 of Sch. 3 to the Betting and Gaming Duties Act 1972. For the meaning of 'society' see below.

GENERAL RULES

Not more than one payment (to include entrance fee, participation fee, payments for cards, etc.) must be made by each player, and no such payment may exceed £1.

The payment must cover all games played at the entertainment (i.e. all bingo games and any other games permitted by s. 41 of the Gaming Act 1968) and the total value of all prizes and awards distributed in respect of those games must not exceed £100.

The whole of the proceeds of these entrance payments, apart from legitimate expenses and permitted expenditure on prizes or awards, must be used for purposes other than private gain. For the meaning of 'private gain' see pages 37 and 50.

The expenses that may be deducted from payments must not exceed the reasonable cost of the facilities provided for the

*Taken with Betting and Gaming Duties Act 1972, Sch. 3, para. 3(1).

purposes of the games.

The public may be admitted (Gaming Act 1968, s. 1(2)(*b*)).

S. 42 of the Gaming Act 1968 does not apply in that this event can be advertised if the provisions of s. 41 are adhered to.

FURTHER RULES RELATING TO A SERIES OF ENTERTAINMENTS

Where two or more entertainments are promoted on the same premises by the same persons on the same day, then the £100 limit on prizes and the rules about proceeds and expenses apply to those entertainments collectively as though they were a single entertainment.

Where, however, a series of entertainments is held otherwise than on the same day, then each entertainment can be treated separately, whether or not some or all of the persons taking part in any one of those entertainments are thereby qualified to take part in any other of them.

If each of the persons taking part in the bingo games played at the final entertainment of the series is qualified to do so because of participation in the bingo games played at another entertainment of the series held on a previous day, then the upper limit for prizes or awards for that final entertainment is £200.

Meaning of 'society'

In order to qualify for exemption as detailed above, a society must be established and conducted either wholly for purposes other than purposes of any commercial undertaking; or wholly or mainly for the purpose of participation in or support of athletic sports or athletic games. This includes any club, institution, organisation or association of persons, by whatever name called, and any separate branch of such a club, institution, organisation or association. (Lotteries and Amusements Act 1976, s. 22(2); Gaming Act 1968, s. 51A; Betting and Gaming Duties Act 1972, Sch. 3, para. 3(3).)

Meaning of 'private gain'

In construing 'private gain' the proceeds of an entertainment promoted on behalf of a society which are applied for any purpose calculated to benefit the society as a whole are not regarded as being used for private gain by reason only that their application for that purpose results in benefit to any person as an individual (Lotteries and Amusements Act 1976, s. 22(1); Gaming Act 1968, s. 51A; Betting and Gaming Duties Act 1972, Sch. 3, para. 3(2)).

5. Pool betting

Pools are big business. In the year ended 31 March 1977, the British hazarded over £260 million in pursuit of those elusive, sometimes golden dividends. It is not surprising that some charities have sought to share in this bonanza. There are, however, some serious disadvantages:

(*a*) The major promoters are well organised and are able to offer huge prizes. It is difficult for smaller 'charity' pools to compete.

(*b*) Some charities, and some members of charities, object to becoming involved with so obvious a form of gambling, and feel that the public image of their organisation suffers more than the financial benefit can justify.

(*c*) Pool betting is normally subject to an excise duty of 40 per cent and to revenue control.

(*d*) Considerable organisation is required, almost certainly necessitating 'outside' help. We have commented on the dangers of this situation elsewhere (notably page 31).

(*e*) The benefit to the charity may be small in relation to the total proceeds. Indeed the pool promoter may derive more benefit from the use of the charity's name than the charity derives from his services.

The term 'pools', in popular parlance, is loosely applied to a wide variety of competitions. For legal purposes we must be more precise, and will have to deal with four categories.

Lotteries

Some so-called 'pools' are really lotteries, in that the participant accepts a chance offered to him or makes a choice which is 'blind'. If the lottery is lawful (see Chapter 3) then it is exempt from pool betting duty (Betting and Gaming Duties Act 1972, s. 6(3)(*b*)).

Pool competitions under the Pool Competitions Act 1971

Before 1971 a number of charities and sporting clubs benefited from competitions organised by independent registered pool promoters. It is said that two of the major charities, Cancer and Polio Research and Spastics, raised over £20 million in this way. A High Court decision, however, found that the way in which a number of such competitions were operated constituted an illegal lottery. This led to the passing of the Pool Competitions Act 1971, to prevent a sudden, probably disastrous loss of income by charities which relied heavily upon this type of fund-raising. The Act made provisions to permit such competitions then already established, to continue to operate under a special Gaming Board licence for a period of five years. The Secretary of State was given power to extend this period, and, at the time of writing, its date of expiry is 26 July 1979.

Only seven pool competitions continue to be run under this special and temporary dispensation.

Competitions held under the provisions of this Act are liable to pool betting duty, but at a special rate of 33⅓ per cent.

Fixed-odds coupon betting

Coupon betting is defined in s. 11 of the Betting and Gaming Duties Act 1972. Bets are deemed to be made by way of coupon betting 'where they are made in pursuance of an invitation which offers stated odds for a choice of bets, being bets of a description not commonly made without such an invitation, unless made by way of pool betting, and not of a description commonly made by means of a totalizator'. Coupon betting at fixed odds is, in fact, outside the legal definition of pool betting, but, nevertheless, pool betting duty extends to it by virtue of s. 6(1)(*b*) of the same Act. The relevant law is extremely complex and its interpretation no easy matter. Since this form of competition is, we believe, of very limited appeal and organised only by bookmakers, we do not propose to trouble our fund-raising readers with further details.

Pool betting

Though commonly associated with football, this is not the only form of pool betting. A legal definition is provided in the Betting and Gaming Duties Act 1972, s. 10(1). Bets are held to be made by way of pool betting wherever a number of persons make bets:

(*a*) On terms that the winnings of such of those persons as are winners, shall be, or be a share of, or be determined by reference to, the stake money paid or agreed to be paid by those persons, whether the bets are made by means of a totalizator, or by filling up and returning coupons or other printed or written forms, or otherwise howsoever, or

(b) on terms that the winnings of such of those persons as are winners shall be, or shall include, an amount (not determined by reference to the stake money paid or agreed to be paid by those persons) which is divisible in any proportions among such of those persons as are winners, or

(c) on the basis that the winners or their winnings shall, to any extent, be at the discretion of the promoter or some other person.

Intending promoters of pool competitions are faced with a number of prior legal obligations.

1. They must apply for registration under Schedule 2 to the Betting, Gaming and Lotteries Act 1963 with the appropriate registering authority (in England, the council of any district or London borough and the Common Council of the City of London; in Scotland, the council of any islands area or district.

2. If registered, they must conduct business to comply with a number of requirements of paragraphs 13–19 of the same schedule, and must render specified information under paragraphs 20–24.

3. They must apply for a permit from HM Customs and Excise for each of the premises used for their business (the application form appears as an appendix to Customs and Excise notice No. 147). The permit, which is free and does not need to be renewed, should not be confused with a bookmaker's permit.

4. They must make an 'entry' of all relevant premises on a prescribed Customs and Excise form.

5. They must notify Customs and Excise of the rules of any competitions which it is intended to promote, any new competitions and any changes in the rules of existing competitions.

6. They must keep records to the satisfaction of Customs and Excise (these are outlined in para. 11 of notice No. 147). The exact form in which these records have to be kept is not prescribed, but Customs and Excise have power to do so if necessary.

7. They must allow access to any officer of Customs and Excise at all reasonable times, allow him to inspect relevant documents, and give him such information and assistance as he may require.

The precise rules governing liability to pool betting duty are set out in notice No. 147, para. 1. The general position is that all bets made by way of pool betting with a promoter who is in Great Britain, i.e. England, Scotland and Wales, are liable to duty at the rate of 40 per cent unless they are such as to be chargeable with the general betting duty. The position in Northern Ireland and the Isle of Man is similar but under their own laws. It is absolutely illegal to operate a betting business or agency for a promoter outside Great Britain, Northern Ireland and the Isle of Man, or to distribute or even to be in possession of an advertisement or other document (e.g. a coupon) relating to such betting.

The duty is payable not only on stake money (without any deductions for commission or expenses whatever), but also on any additional payments relating to the bet, unless the promoter can prove that they are neither expenses nor profits. There is, however, an important exception in favour of donations to charity or sport. Pool betting duty is not charged on payments made by punters which are for the benefit of and passed on to a society established and conducted for charitable purposes only, or wholly or mainly for the support of athletic sports or athletic games and not for purposes of private gain, provided that the punters know, when making the payments, that their purpose is to benefit the society. (Betting and Gaming Duties Act 1972, s. 7(4). A 'society' includes any club, institution, organisation or association of persons, by whatever name called.)

Punters in a 'charity' pool might pay 5p a week, out of a total payment of 20p, as a donation to a named recognised charity. Provided that the promoter passes the sum total of the 5p donations to the named charity, relief from duty can be claimed on the amount, but not on any additional amount which he might choose to donate to the charity.

We recognise that the law relating to pools and similar competitions is extremely complex; indeed we are convinced that involvement in the organisation of pool betting is not for the amateur. However, we hope that those who are interested in this form of fund-raising will now be better able to consider joint ventures with registered pool promoters.

Filmed racing

A number of commercial firms provide films of horse or greyhound racing for use by clubs and charities. They consist of a parade of the runners followed by the race – usually from an overseas racetrack. They are intended to provide entertainment and to raise money – to 'have fun with fund-raising' as one advertiser puts it. But there is an important legal qualification. If money is staked and accepted *before* any of the film is shown and without giving the filmgoers sufficient information to make a positive act of selection, and the film is then shown *without interruption*, then the stakes will not be bets at all and will not therefore be liable to any form of betting duty. Such arrangements would, however, constitute a lottery and as such would need to conform with the Lotteries and Amusements Act 1976 (see Chapter 3).

If, on the other hand, the film is stopped between the parade and the race and money taken then, and if the parade is sufficiently informative for the filmgoers to exercise some judgement, punters will be making a positive act of selection, and the stakes will become liable to pool betting duty as bets made by means of a totalizator not on an approved racetrack.

6. Other gaming

Gaming machines

In the right place – such as a social club which regularly attracts members in some numbers – a gaming machine can prove to be a steady source of funds. Gaming machines in members' clubs are normally supplied on hire, and s. 28 of the Gaming Act 1968 requires the hiring charge to be a fixed periodic amount determined in advance (i.e. it may not be supplied on profit-sharing terms). The amount of the hiring charges will vary enormously according to age and type of machine supplied, the amount of wear and tear the machine is likely to suffer, the frequency with which it is required to be changed, and whether the supplier pays the licence duty, etc. Machines can be purchased outright, but few clubs choose to do so.

As with other forms of gambling, the legal requirements, both social and revenue, are of some complexity. Basically, no gaming machine may be made available on any premises except in certain circumstances and under certain conditions which are prescribed in the Gaming Act 1968. We do not propose to deal with all of these, but restrict our explanations to those areas which we believe to be relevant to our purpose. It is, however, first necessary to define what is meant by a gaming machine. For the purposes of the Gaming Act 1968, a gaming machine is one which is constructed or adapted for playing a game of chance by means of the machine, and which has a slot or other aperture for the insertion of money, in cash or money's worth in the form of tokens. (A game of chance includes a game which combines both skill and chance or pretends to do so, and the fact that a game contains an element of skill does not prevent it from being treated as a game of chance if nothing but superlative skill can overcome the element of chance.) Such machines may, or may not, be liable to gaming machine licence duty under the Betting and Gaming Duties Act 1972.

A machine is *liable* to duty if the outcome of the game is determined by the action of the machine (whether or not provision is made for manipulation of the machine by the player).

A machine is *not liable* to duty if it is constructed or adapted so that where a person plays it once and successfully he receives:

(*a*) Nothing save an opportunity to play again (once or more often) without further payment; or

(*b*) by the automatic action of the machine either a money prize not greater than the amount payable to play the machine once, or a token or tokens which are exchangeable only for such a money prize.

Such machines are commonly called 'amusement only' machines, and plainly have no fund-raising potential. Although gaming machines for the purposes of the Gaming Act, they are not treated as gaming machines for the purposes of the duty.

Among the circumstances in which dutiable machines are permitted to be made available for play are the following.

Members' clubs (Gaming Act 1968, s. 30, s. 31)

Under Part 3 of the Act, bona-fide members' clubs may install gaming machines, provided that they apply for and are granted registration under Sch. 7 (England and Wales) or Sch. 8 (Scotland) to the Act.

The forms of application are set out in the Gaming Act (Registration under Part III) Regulations 1969 and the Gaming Act (Registration under Part III) (Scotland) Regulations 1969 respectively. In England and Wales, applications are dealt with by the local licensing justices and in Scotland by the local sheriff.

The essential conditions are that not more than two machines are made available for play and never when the public has access to the premises, that it must not cost more than 10p to play once, and that no one may receive or be entitled to receive any article, benefit or advantage except a coin or coins delivered by the machine. The machine itself must display a statement of the value of the prize(s) for playing once, any circumstances in which the prize(s) cannot be won, and a statement of the minimum percentage payout. At present, there is no limit on the amount paid out by machines used under the conditions of section 31 of the Act, and they are therefore commonly referred to as 'jackpot' machines.

Such machines are subject to gaming machine (excise) licence duty, the duty depending on the number of machines and the cost of playing them once, as follows:

Type of machine	One machine	Two machines
Costing 1¼p or less to play once	£ 50 (whole year) £ 27.50 (½ year)	£150 (whole year) £ 82.50 (½ year)
Costing more than 1¼p to play once	£100 (whole year) £ 55 (½ year)	£300 (whole year) £165 (½ year)

Applications for licences on Customs and Excise form L21 (available from local Customs and Excise or Collectors' offices) must be made at least 14 days before the gaming machines are first made available for play. The form and appropriate remittance should be sent to the Collector of Customs and Excise in whose area the premises are situated. Further details are given in Customs and Excise Notice 454 and the relevant legislation is contained in the Betting and Gaming Duties Act 1972, s. 21 to 27 and Sch. 4 to 7 (as amended).

Machines used incidentally to entertainments (Gaming Act 1968, s. 33, s. 51A; Betting and Gaming Duties Act 1972, Sch. 4, para. 1)

Machines may be used at bazaars, sales of work, fêtes and similar entertainments, exempt from gaming machine licence duty, provided that the opportunity to win prizes by the machines, with or without any other facilities for gaming is not the only or the only substantial inducement for people to attend. In other words, the machine must be only an incidental attraction. The whole proceeds of the entertainment (including the proceeds of gaming by means of any machine) apart from legitimate expenses, must be devoted to purposes other than private gain (which has the same construction as previously explained on page 44). Expenses may include those incurred in connection with the provision of gaming machines and prizes, but if a hiring charge for the use of a machine depends in any way on the extent to which it (or some other machine) is used, then the hire charge is held to be an application of the proceeds to private gain. Such a hire charge could not therefore be legitimately deducted as expenses.

Value added tax is chargeable on the takings of gaming machines. A gaming machine for VAT purposes is defined in the Finance (No. 2) Act 1975, s. 21. Takings from gaming machines which are outside this definition because they do not involve games of chance are nevertheless taxable. Full details are given in Customs and Excise leaflet No. 15/75/VLC available from local VAT offices. The implications for voluntary organisations and charities are more fully explained in Chapter 8.

Amusements with prizes

We touched on this subject in Chapter 4 in relation to bingo. The legislation (Lotteries and Amusements Act 1976, s. 15) extends, however, to the provision of many other forms of 'amusements with prizes' at bazaars, sales of work, fêtes, dinners, dances, sporting or athletic events and similar entertainments. It applies, in fact, to any lottery or gaming which does *not* constitute:

(a) gaming under Part 2 of the Gaming Act 1968 (gaming on premises licensed or registered under that part of the Act), or

(b) gaming by means of machine under Part 3 of the Gaming Act 1968. Gaming machines are, however, allowed at such events under the provisions of the Gaming Act 1968, s. 33 (see page 52).

The following conditions must be observed:

(a) the whole proceeds of the entertainment, after deducting the expenses of the entertainment, must be devoted to purposes other than private gain (see page 44); and

(b) the facilities for winning prizes at the amusements, with or without any other facilities offered for taking part in lotteries or gaming, must not be the only, or the only substantial, inducement to persons to attend the entertainment.

Expenses may include those incurred in connection with the provision of gaming and prizes, but as with the provision of gaming machines, if a hiring charge for the use of any equipment needed for holding a lottery or gaming at the entertainment depends in any way on the extent to which it (or some other equipment) is used, then the hire charge is held to be an application of the proceeds of the entertainment to private gain. Such a hire charge could not therefore be legitimately deducted as expenses.

Prize competitions

Under s. 14 of the Lotteries and Amusements Act 1976 it is *illegal* to conduct the following types of competition in or through any newspaper; in connection with any trade or business (apart from pool betting carried on by someone whose only trade is that of a bookmaker); in connection with the sale of any article to the public.

1. Any competition in which prizes are offered for forecasts of the result of either;
    (*a*) a future event; or
    (*b*) a past event the result of which is not yet ascertained, or not yet generally known.
2. Any other competition in which success does not depend to a substantial degree on the exercise of skill.

It follows, however, that those competitions which do call for a substantial degree of skill are permissible, and indeed are familiar in the popular press and on the packaging of well known products.

7. Tax reliefs

Charities quite rightly enjoy special privileges in respect of internal direct taxation, for instance a large measure of relief from corporation tax and income tax. These privileges reflect the high esteem with which our charities are regarded, and serve as an official acknowledgement of the benefits these organisations afford our society as a whole. However, many people feel that these tax concessions do not go far enough and do not provide the degree of encouragement to charitable giving which is merited. In particular, the covenant relief arrangements are criticised for not providing the necessary spur to potential donors who pay tax at the higher rates, because the benefit to the charity is restricted to recovery of only the basic rate of tax. It is also widely considered that the covenant period – which must exceed six years – is too long, and that, in addition, the machinery for recovering tax is unduly cumbersome. Our concern in this book is not with the position which might be considered desirable, but rather with things as they are.

Income tax exemption

Exemption from income tax is afforded to legitimate charities on a wide, indeed almost complete, front. The specific exemptions are set out in the Income and Corporation Taxes Act 1970, s. 360(1) as follows:

The following exemptions shall be granted on a claim in that behalf to the Board —

(a) exemption from tax under Schedules A and D in respect of the rents and profits of any lands, tenements, hereditaments or heritages belonging to a hospital, public school or almshouse, or vested in trustees for charitable purposes, so far as the same are applied to charitable purposes only,

(b) exemption from tax under Schedule B in respect of any lands occupied by a charity,

   (*c*) exemption —
      (i) from tax under Schedule C in respect of any interest, annuities, dividends or shares of annuities;
      (ii) from tax under Schedule D in respect of any yearly interest or other annual payment,* and
      (iii) from tax under Schedule F in respect of any distribution, where the income in question forms part of the income of a charity, or is, according to rules or regulations established by Act of Parliament, charter, decree, deed of trust or will, applicable to charitable purposes only, and so far as it is applied to charitable purposes only,

   (*d*) exemption from tax under Schedule C in respect of any interest, annuities, dividends or shares of annuities which are in the names of trustees and are applicable solely towards the repairs of any cathedral, college, church or chapel, or of any building used solely for the purpose of divine worship, so far as the same are applied to those purposes,

   (*e*) exemption from tax under Schedule D in respect of the profits of any trade carried on by a charity, if the profits are applied solely to the purposes of the charity and either —
      (i) the trade is exercised in the course of the actual carrying out of a primary purpose of the charity, or
      (ii) the work in connection with the trade is mainly carried out by beneficiaries of the charity.

In the context of fund-raising, our primary concern is with the exemption afforded under s. 360(1)(*e*) to the profits of trade. It is apparent that this applies only in limited circumstances, and that wider trading activities by charities are therefore liable to tax. This liability is, however, ameliorated in practice in three ways:

   1. There is an extra-statutory concession (C5 in Inland Revenue booklet IR1) in respect of the profits of trading by voluntary organisations to raise funds for charity at bazaars, jumble sales, carnivals, gymkhanas and similar activities. Tax is not charged on such profits provided the following conditions are satisfied:
      (*a*) the organisation is not regularly trading
      (*b*) the trading is not in competition with other traders
      (*c*) the activities are supported substantially because the

---

Authors' note: the provision is extended by an extra-statutory concession (B9 in Inland Revenue Booklet IR1) to bank interest and discounts on Treasury Bills. This and other similar concessions are of general application, but it must be borne in mind that in a particular case there may be special circumstances to be taken into account in considering their application.

public are aware that any profits will be devoted to charity (d) the profits are transferred to charities or otherwise applied for charitable purposes.

2. Charities who trade on any scale may decide (and many do) to entrust their non-exempt trading activities to a separate limited company. The trading subsidiary enters into a deed of covenant effective for more than six years and transfers its profits under that covenant. Tax must be deducted at the basic rate and paid to the Inland Revenue, but the charity, if recognised as such by the Inland Revenue, is entitled to reclaim the tax. This is more fully explained later in this chapter.

3. The resale of gifts in kind may be outside the scope of the tax. It cannot be said that merely because something is given to a vendor the proceeds of subsequent sale are not receipts of his trade (the 'rag and bone' man or the scrap metal dealer is frequently 'given' things in the sense that he pays nothing for them, but they are received by him in the course of his trade and the proceeds are receipts of his trade). But there are some circumstances in which donated goods can be sold by charities without incurring liability to corporation tax. This principally affects charity shops, where the practical position is that the Inland Revenue is prepared to leave out of account items that represent pure donations so long as the shop can and does identify such *genuine gifts*. So what is a 'genuine gift', and a 'pure donation' in this context? There seem to be three possibilities:

(a) An individual may say, in effect, 'If you sell this for me you may keep (say) half the proceeds.' In that case, the shop's share is received in consideration of providing a service, i.e. for effecting the sale, and is a trading receipt and as such liable to tax.

(b) Or he may say, 'I have a number of things which are in my way. If you will take them off my hands you can have them for nothing.' Again there is an element of service. The individual may have preferred the charity to enjoy the proceeds, rather than (say) the local scrap merchant, but he did not act with the sole motive of making a donation to charity.

(c) The genuine gift, for tax purposes, arises when the donor says, in effect, 'I wish to make a donation, but not in cash. Here is a saleable item for you to sell.' In that event the proceeds of the sale may be left out of account. But it is important to appreciate that where a sale is so treated, the related costs of selling (i.e. a proportion of the costs of running the shop, as well as any direct costs of repair etc. to make the item more readily saleable) are equally outside the course of trade and cannot be claimed as deduction in computing tax on the proceeds of the shop as a whole. It is as though the donor had made a cash gift equal in amount to the proceeds minus the costs incurred in selling it.

Covenanted gifts

Dispositions under a deed of covenant, for a period exceeding six calendar years, whether made by individuals or companies, are treated for tax purposes as the income of the *recipient*. If the recipient is a charity recognised by the Inland Revenue, and thus exempt from tax on such income, it may reclaim tax at the basic rate paid by the donor on the covenanted amount. With a basic rate of 33 per cent, this means that for each £67 received from donors who have themselves paid tax when *they* received the money, the charity can reclaim £33 (= 33 per cent of (£67 + £33)) thus enhancing donations by nearly 50 per cent. (Tax relief for charitable covenants is allowable *only* at the basic rate regardless of whether the donor paid a higher tax rate or the investment surcharge.)

This is a very significant source of additional income, having the added advantage of being regular and certain, but is often neglected by charities, who are perhaps reluctant to grasp the nettle of the necessary administrative procedures and are slow to encourage and educate potential and existing donors. Our feeling is that the complexities of the system are exaggerated, and that most potential donors likely to participate will be well able to understand the principles involved if trouble is taken to explain them. Appeals for covenanted gifts must, of course, be promoted with discretion. To ask a possible supporter, not specially sympathetic to your cause, for a seven-year commitment may well be counter-productive! But if only the more significant existing supporters can be persuaded to covenant their donations, the financial benefit can be considerable.

Donors enter into a deed of covenant with the charity in which they undertake to pay a certain amount annually for a stipulated period (usually seven years or until previous death and usually by banker's order for convenience).

The amount may be:

1. A specified gross sum (from which the donor deducts basic-rate tax); in this case the charity will always receive the same amount though the proportions attributable to the donor and to reclaimed tax may vary with changes of rate.
2. Such a sum as will provide a specified amount after deduction of tax at the basic rate for the time being in force; here the amount actually paid by the donor will be constant but the amounts of tax reclaimed will vary as the tax rate changes.
3. A percentage of income, either gross or net; this is particularly appropriate where the donor has a fluctuating income, perhaps in the form of fees, profits or royalties, and does not wish to commit himself to a fixed amount.

Normally, donations under deed of covenant are made by those who already pay tax at the standard rate on an amount at least equal to the gross sum covenanted. The donor deducts tax at the standard rate from the gross amount of the payments he makes under the deed and is required to account to the Inland Revenue for the tax so deducted.

To satisfy the law, the covenant need only be *capable* of surviving for more than six years. It is therefore open to donors to stipulate special conditions, e.g. 'subject to my continuing to be employed as a civil servant'.

It is also desirable that the covenant should include a provision that it will lapse if the covenantor dies before the full term has been completed. Another important point is that the donation must be pure income to the charity, not a payment for goods, services or other benefits.

Dispositions by companies made under the conditions described above generally enjoy a greater measure of tax relief. The company is allowed to deduct the *gross* amount paid under the covenant from its profits in calculating its liability to corporation tax. It deducts tax *at the basic rate* from the gross amount donated and accounts for this to the Inland Revenue. The balance is paid to the charity, which reclaims the tax previously deducted.

Thus, with corporation tax at 42 per cent and a basic rate of 33 per cent, if the company pays £100 gross, it escapes corporation tax of £42, pays basic rate tax of £33 and pays the charity £67. The net cost to the company is thus £58 while the charity receives £100.

If, however, a company has no liability to corporation tax, it must nevertheless pay tax at the basic rate on the gross donation.

The cost to the company of a £100 gross donation is then, in fact, the full £100.

In the case of close companies (very broadly speaking, those companies which are under the control of five or fewer persons or are under the control of their directors), the amount donated may be treated by the Inland Revenue as though it was the income of the participators and apportioned among them for tax purposes. Then, if their personal tax rates exceed the basic rate paid on the donation they may be personally charged to tax at the rate of that excess. We understand, however, that such apportionments are relatively uncommon in practice.

Technically, this close-company provision applies equally to a charity's wholly owned trading companies, but provided that there are no other participators in the companies concerned, no apportionment would in practice be made.

Procedures

A specimen form for completion by a donor is shown in Figure 7.1.

In support of a charity's claim for repayment of income tax, the covenanter is asked to give a certificate on form R 185(AP). This certificate states the gross amount he has paid, the amount of income tax deducted, and on it the covenantor certifies that he has paid or will pay this amount of tax to the Inland Revenue. Whilst a form R 185(AP) is required in all cases in respect of a first claim under a deed, it can normally be dispensed with for subsequent years if the amount covenanted does not exceed £30 net, provided that prior approval is obtained from the Inland Revenue, Claims Branch, Charity Division, Magdalen House, Trinity Road, Bootle, Merseyside L69 9BB, who will advise the relevant conditions.

Claims are made on form R235A. Additional schedules are provided on form R 248 (where the number of 'over £30' covenantors exceeds 50) and forms R 248A and R 248A (summary) (listing 'not exceeding £30' covenantors). Each deed of covenant should be sent with the claim which contains the first payment under it. (Covenants by companies must have been given under the seal of the company, those by partnerships must have been signed by all partners.) Similarly, detailed accounts showing the income and expenditure of the charity for the period for which the claim is made and copies of any printed reports issued should be submitted.

Covenantors should be advised to enter the gross amount payable under the deed as 'outgoings' on the space provided on their own income tax returns.

Law

Sections 52 and 53 of the Income and Corporation Taxes Act 1970 deal with deduction of tax, though payments by companies always come within s. 53. Where a payer (other than a company) has sufficient income which is chargeable to tax to cover the gross sum payable he can deduct and retain income tax at the basic rate in force on the date the payment is *due*. If the income which is chargeable to tax is less than the gross payment, income tax should be deducted at the basic rate in force on the date the payment is *made*.

If a payment falls within s. 52, then s. 3 of the Income and Corporation Taxes Act 1970 provides that so much of the payer's income, equal to the amount of the payment, as may be deducted in computing his total income, shall be charged at the basic rate. If a payment falls within s. 53, then s. 53(2) similarly provides that tax at the basic rate shall be charged on the payer on an amount equal to the amount of the payment. The accounting to the Inland Revenue for the tax deducted by companies from payments under deeds of covenant is provided for in s. 53(4) of the Income and Corporation Taxes Act 1970.

Ss. 434 and 445(1) of the Act concern dispositions which cannot exceed six years and revocable settlements. Their effect, taken with related case law, is that dispositions (unless made for 'valuable and sufficient consideration') of any income chargeable with tax under Income Tax Acts for the benefit of another person for a period which can exceed six calendar years are regarded for all the purposes of the Income Tax Acts to be the income of the recipient. A 'disposition' in this context includes any trust, covenant, agreement or arrangement but it must be irrevocable within the stipulated period.

Loans

A donor may wish to make a lump-sum donation to a charity, perhaps in response to an immediate urgent need for funds. Its value can be substantially enhanced if instead he transfers the money as an interest-free loan, repayable in equal instalments over seven or more years, and at the same time enters into a separate covenant agreement to pay the same sum to the charity over the same period. Thus the charity will benefit by the total sum at once and there will be no further effective cost to it or the donor because the covenant payments will exactly redress the loan and vice versa.

Deed of Covenant

I (full christian and surnames in block capitals)_____

_____

of (address in block capitals)_____

_____

hereby covenant with Voluntary Service Overseas, whose
registered office is at 9 Belgrave Square, London SW1X 8PW,
for a period of (1)   years from the date hereof or
during my life (whichever shall be the shorter) I will pay
annually to the said Voluntary Service Overseas such sum as
shall, after deduction of Income Tax at the standard rate for
the time being in force, leave in the hands of the said Voluntary
Service Overseas the net sum of (2) £   , such sum
to be paid from my general fund of taxed income so that I shall
receive no personal or private benefit in either of the said periods
from the above mentioned annual sum or any part thereof. In
witness whereof I have hereunto set my hand and seal this

(3)_____day of_____19_____
Signed, sealed and delivered by the said Covenantor. (4)

Signature of Covenantor_____ (LS)

Signature of Witness_____

Address of Witness_____

_____

_____

Occupation of Witness_____

1 The minimum number of years is 7, but any greater number is
permissible.
2 Insert the actual amount you wish to give each year, not the gross
amount VSO will receive after Income Tax has been recovered.
3 This date must be earlier than the date of the first payment given on
the Banker's Order.
4 The deed should be executed in the presence of a witness who must
also sign in the space provided. LS as printed means that no other seal
or sealing is necessary.
5 VSO makes the necessary arrangements with the Board of Inland
Revenue for the recovery of tax.

Figure 7.1 Multi-purpose form, incorporating a 'net' deed
of covenant, used by Voluntary Service Overseas

Donation

I enclose a donation to Voluntary Service Overseas for the sum of

£ _____

Name (block capitals) _____

_____

Address (block capitals) _____

_____

_____

Signed _____ Date _____

Banker's Order

To (name and address of Bank) _____

_____

Please pay to the account of Voluntary Service Overseas
(A/c No 71026348) at the Midland Bank, 19 Grosvenor Place,
Hyde Park Corner, London SW1X 7HT (Code No 40-03-17),
the sum of

£ _____ on _____ next, and
annually thereafter on the same date for the succeeding *years.

Name (block capitals) _____

Address (block capitals) _____

_____

_____

Signed _____ Date _____

*Insert nine if a 10-year covenant or six if a 7-year covenant.
To be sent with the Deed of Covenant, or may be used for a non-
covenanted annual payment.

Fig. 7.1 (cont'd)

(The loan repayments and covenant payments must be actual and separate transactions.) The charity will also benefit by reclaiming tax on the covenanted annual payments. *This procedure cannot be applied retrospectively to outright donations.*

There are, of course, some disadvantages – a certain amount of administrative headache which may only be worth while if the sums involved are reasonably substantial, and the fact that in the absence of a special capital need many charities would prefer a regular income to a lump sum.

Another loan arrangement, this time without a parallel covenant, is particularly suitable to donors in the higher income bracket. If a taxpayer who pays tax at 83 per cent on a proportion of his income invests £1000 at say 7 per cent, then he receives interest of £70 but may pay tax on this of £58. Thus his real income from the investment is only £12. If, however, he lends £1000 free of interest to a registered charity, which invests the money at 7 per cent then the charity derives £70 which forms part of its tax-free income. Thus a sacrifice of only £12 of real income yields £70 to the charity. The principle holds good for taxpayers paying tax at lower rates, but the ratio of cost to benefit is, of course, reduced.

All the methods of giving described in this section presuppose, indeed demand, efficient administration and office routine on the part of the charity, and the cost of this must be balanced against the benefits derived. If the work involved is a problem, charities may wish to enlist the services of the Charities Aid Foundation, 48 Pembury Road, Tonbridge, Kent TN9 2JD. This foundation, which now enjoys the patronage of the Duke of Edinburgh, was established in its original form in 1924 as part of the National Council of Social Service. Since 1974, it has operated independently, developing a range of services to encourage and facilitate the distribution of money to charities. These include a complete service to charities which lack the necessary resources to administer an effective deed-of-covenant system, including the recovery of tax and maintenance of suitable records. Full details are available on application. The charges are modest: 75p for each deed registered, and an operating charge of 75p per deed per annum. However, if less than 20 deeds are in operation there is normally a minimum charge of £15, and if a deed is paid by instalments, the operating charge of 75p is subject to a surcharge of £3 per annum.

Charitable and benevolent gifts by traders

The Income and Corporation Taxes Act 1970, s. 411(8) provides that, in general, the cost of gifts is not an admissible deduction in computing profits chargeable under Schedule D nor in management expenses claims. However, expenditure on gifts is not regarded as within this provision, provided that:

(a) it is allowable under s. 130(a) of the same Act; and

(b) is made for the benefit of a body or association of persons established for educational, cultural, religious, recreational or benevolent purposes when that body or association is:

    (i) local in relation to the donor's business activities, and

    (ii) not restricted to persons connected with the donor; and

(c) the expenditure is 'reasonably small' in relation to the scale of the donor's business.

This relief applies both to individual traders and to companies (Booklet IR1).

Capital gains tax

Capital gains tax is not chargeable on capital gains made by a recognised charity which are applicable and applied for charitable purposes (Income and Corporation Taxes Act 1970, s. 360(2) and Finance Act 1965, s. 35(1)). Nor is a donor liable to such tax in respect of property which he gives to a recognised charity (Finance Act 1972, s. 119).

Capital transfer tax

Legacies

Throughout the length and breadth of this country, thousands of people are dying to help charities, if you see what we mean. This posthumous beneficence is necessarily irregular and unpredictable but hardly less welcome for that. Legacies can provide a steady and significant source of funds, and some charities receive the greater part of their income in this way. It is, of course, a delicate area, and appeals must be made with tact and discretion. Nobody particularly likes to be reminded of death. On the other hand, most of us are able to take a certain pleasure in allocating our worldly goods to the time when we will have no further use for them and to a cause which has captured our imagination and concern during our lives. There is a definite satisfaction in knowing that our money will go on serving a purpose which we consider to be useful. This is a powerful and genuine argument for charitable bequests and one which can be appealed to with the greatest sincerity and conviction. Another powerful persuasion is the fact that tax relief has been much improved in recent years. Bequests to recognised charities of up to £100,000 are now normally exempt from capital transfer tax. To appreciate the effect of this it is necessary to understand the normal basis on which the tax is charged. At the time of writing, an estate is 'banded' for tax as follows:

The first	£25,000	nil
The next	£5,000	10%
The next	£5,000	15%
The next	£5,000	20%
The next	£10,000	25%
The next	£10,000	30%
The next	£10,000	35%
The next	£20,000	40%
The next	£20,000	45%
The next	£20,000	50%
The next	£30,000	55%
The next	£350,000	60%
The next	£500,000	65%
The next	£1,000,000	70%
Thereafter		75%

So let us say that Smith leaves a taxable estate of £75,000 and Jones £42,000. The respective charges would be:

Smith				£	Jones				£
£25,000	@	0%	=	nil	£25,000	@	0%	=	nil
£ 5,000	@	10%	=	500	£ 5,000	@	10%	=	500
£ 5,000	@	15%	=	750	£ 5,000	@	15%	=	750
£ 5,000	@	20%	=	1000	£ 5,000	@	20%	=	1000
£10,000	@	25%	=	2500	£ 2,000	@	25%	=	500
£10,000	@	30%	=	3000					
£10,000	@	35%	=	3500					
£ 5,000	@	40%	=	2000					
£75,000				£13250	£42,000				£2750

Now let us suppose that Smith has bequeathed £6000 tax-free to charity and Jones has similarly bequeathed £4000. The effect is to reduce their taxable estates by those respective amounts. The tax due upon Smith's estate is reduced by £2350 (£5000 @ 40% and £1000 @ 35%), while that of Jones is reduced by £900 (£2000 @ 25%, and £2000 @ 20%). We hope that this is clear. It will be apparent that the tax saving depends very much on the overall size of the estate.

We said that bequests to recognised charities up to £100,000 are *normally* exempt from tax. There are, however, some exc' ~tions. These are set out in the Finance Act 1975, Sch. 6, para. 15 (as amended by the Finance Act 1976, Part 4).

The main (but not the only) exceptions are:

1. Where a bequest is made conditional upon some event and that condition has not been satisfied within 12 months after the transfer.

2. Where a bequest passes to the charity only after an intermediate interest in favour of someone else. *This does not, however, extend to intermediate life interests.* Where a bequest is made in the form of a life interest to person X, passing on his death to a recognised charity, then the eventual transfer to the charity is considered *in relation to the death of person X* and thus will be wholly exempt from capital transfer tax provided that the bequest together with any other charitable bequests made by X in his own right do not exceed £100,000. Moreover, if the life interest is in favour of the testator's spouse, assuming that both spouses are domiciled in the United Kingdom, then no capital transfer tax would normally be payable on the transfer of the interest to the spouse (Finance Act 1975, Sch. 6, para. 1).

A charity seeking income from bequests will probably wish to appeal in the first instance to existing donors and supporters, bringing to their attention how much a legacy can benefit the cause to which they are already commited, and, given that their estate will attract capital transfer tax, how the charity rather than the state can benefit. It is desirable to give examples to illustrate the tax advantages at various levels. Charities would also be well advised to include information about legacies in their general advertising and literature. It is particularly important to bring the name of the charity and its needs to the notice of solicitors. They are often asked, when preparing wills for clients, for advice on a suitable 'good cause'. More specifically there are a number of people who need a solicitor's guidance in identifying the charity which is most in tune with their sympathies – those, for example, who have lost relatives from a particular disease and wish to help a charity which is committed to finding a cure for it, or those who have a general wish to benefit disabled people or medical research but have no specific organisation in mind.

In making a will, normal principles apply to charitable bequests as to other bequests, but it is important to be aware (and for solicitors to know) that in some circumstances tax exemption can be lost. Bequests may be:

(*a*) a straightforward stipulated amount;

(*b*) reversionary – that is, passing to the charity only after a life interest in favour of another person (often the testator's spouse);

(*c*) residual – that is, the residue or a part of the residue of the estate after bequests to others;

(*d*) contingent – that is, conditional upon some event, for example a named beneficiary predeceasing the testator.

In its simplest form, a charitable bequest can be expressed: 'I bequeath to —— of —— a legacy of £—— free of tax and I declare that the receipt of the treasurer or other authorised officer of —— shall be a sufficient discharge for the same.' But wills are legal documents, and complications can arise for executors if, through lack of expert knowledge, the words used do not convey their intended meaning or omit some vital qualification. Apart from scope for error in the body of the will, the form and acts of attestation and witnessing present dangers to the uninitiated; all or any of these factors may frustrate the intentions of the testator. Our emphatic advice, particularly where there is a bequest to charity, is to urge potential donors to employ a solicitor in drawing up their wills.

The law on tax and bequests is contained in the Finance Act 1975, Sch. 6 as amended by the Finance Act 1976, Part 4.

Para. 1	Transfers between spouses
Para.10	Gifts to charities
Para.11	Gifts to political parties
Para.12	Gifts for national purposes
Para.13	Gifts for public benefit
Para.15	Exceptional circumstances

In respect of legacies, para. 10(1) exempts from capital transfer tax 'transfers of value' that are attributable to property given to charities up to a value of £100,000. Property is regarded as having been given to charities if it becomes the property of charities or is held in trust for charitable purposes only. The expressions 'charity' and 'charitable purposes' are defined in the Income and Corporation Taxes Act 1970, s. 360(3) and have been the subject of a considerable amount of case law over the years. One essential qualification is that the charity must be established in the United Kingdom.

Lifetime dispositions

Gifts made to charity during life are exempt from capital transfer tax on the subsequent death of the donor as follows:

made more than 12 months before death – exempt, regardless of amount;

made in the 12 months before death – exempt up to £100,000 (any excess is therefore liable to capital transfer tax)

See the Finance Act 1975, Sch. 6, para. 10.

8. Value added tax

This chapter is not intended to be a comprehensive guide to value added tax as it affects charities and voluntary organisations. To make it so would be to obscure its primary objectives, which are to explain the broad principles of the tax and to guide fund-raisers on how the law might affect their activities. For those who wish to go deeper, there is really no substitute for the official Customs and Excise notices and the law itself, but an excellent summary guide has been prepared by the National Council of Social Services, 26 Bedford Square, London WC1B 3HU.

VAT is chargeable on most supplies of goods and services in the United Kingdom by a 'taxable person' in the course of business carried on by him. There is no general exemption or relief in favour of voluntary organisations or charities, but there are some specific reliefs for charitable supplies and, like any small business, if the 'taxable turnover' of a voluntary organisation or charity falls below and is unlikely to exceed the statutory limit for registration (currently £10,000 per annum) then there is no requirement to register for VAT purposes and hence no further involvement in the tax beyond the payment of VAT on purchases of taxable goods and services.

Taxable turnover

This term embraces all taxable business supplies whether of goods or of services. The fact that such supplies are made to beneficiaries in pursuit of a charity's objects does not in itself exclude them from VAT. Nor, under present legislation, does the fact that the proceeds of such supplies are used for charitable purposes. In general, if the goods and services are supplied in return for a consideration, they are regarded as being supplied by way of business and therefore taxable. It is noteworthy, however, that the Goodman Committee's recent report, *Charity Law and Voluntary Organisations*, recommended that 'no activity in furtherance of a

70

charity's primary purpose should be considered as business for VAT'.

There are many kinds of taxable turnover; the following are merely examples which seem to us most likely to occur in fund-raising activities and are by no means exhaustive:

1. The proceeds (not just the profit) from:

    (a) the sale of taxable goods and services (*including those carrying a zero rate of tax*);

    (b) charges for admission to entertainments, bazaars, etc.;

    (c) charges for the taxable provision of catering. In some circumstances, catering may be exempt from tax, or 'outside the scope' of VAT when supplied substantially below cost (e.g. 'Meals on Wheels').

2. Net takings from amusement machines, juke-boxes and gaming machines (see Customs and Excise leaflet 15/75/VLC for details).

Many activities of charities, however, are already accepted as not being carried on 'in the course of business' and are accordingly regarded as being outside the scope of VAT. These include voluntary services given free of charge in pursuit of a charity's objects, supplies made to 'distressed' persons at substantially below cost for the relief of their 'distress', and the whole or part of membership subscriptions (for full details see Customs and Excise leaflet VLD/9/76).

As far as fund-raising is concerned, the significant 'non-business' area is that of voluntary contributions, for example donations (including income tax recovered from covenanted donations), bequests, the proceeds of street and house-to-house collections and receipts (other than payments for goods or services) from legally independent trading companies and other fund-raising organisations. The principle is quite straightforward. To be regarded as outside the scope of VAT, the contribution must be entirely optional.

Thus, if badges are sold for an obligatory, specified sum, the proceeds are taxable, whereas emblems which are distributed by charities in token recognition of voluntary donations received from the public are 'outside the scope'.

The treatment of the proceeds of charity entertainments is particularly interesting. The admission charge is clearly taxable, but if a collection is taken up in addition, then, provided that no contribution is specified and there is a free choice to give or not as one sees fit, any voluntary contributions received are not taxable.

The basic charge which permits admission to the function must not be less than the normal commercial price. If there is no such norm – in the case, say, of a ball or dance – then the receipts from the stipulated minimum charges must be sufficient at least to cover all the expenses of the function. All literature and advertising material must make absolutely clear that people who pay only the minimum admission charge will be admitted to the function and where applicable to the appropriate part of the auditorium without having to make any further payment.

Unconditional grants are similarly 'outside the scope', but where the grant is made for the benefit of a named recipient or for some specific purpose which is clearly of benefit to the person or body making the grant, the grant is regarded as being 'the payment for a supply in the course of business' and is therefore taxable.

Registration

Any charity or voluntary organisation which makes taxable supplies of goods or services in the course of business and has a taxable turnover which exceeds or is likely to exceed the statutory limit must apply for VAT registration. There is an obligation to notify Customs and Excise if taxable turnover at the start of each calendar quarter (1 January, April, July and October) exceeded £3500 for the past quarter, £6000 for the past two quarters, £8500 for the past three quarters or, of course, £10,000 for the past year.

Once registered, there is an obligation to account for and pay VAT on the organisation's taxable supplies ('outputs'), and a corresponding entitlement to reclaim (with certain exceptions, e.g. tax on the purchase of motor cars, and certain expenses for business entertaining) VAT which the organisation is charged for goods and services obtained in connection with its *business* activities ('inputs').

In simple terms, output tax is charged on takings and input tax reclaimed on expenses.

If a charity's supplies are predominantly zero-rated, so that they have very few 'outputs' which bear tax, it may actually benefit from registration in that it will nevertheless be able to reclaim tax on its *business* 'inputs' including those relating to zero-rated supplies. In such circumstances, a charity may apply to be registered even though its taxable turnover is below the £10,000 annual limit. It is a question of balancing any financial benefit against the administration cost and nuisance of meeting the official requirements connected with VAT. A similar situation may arise where a charity receives a large part of its income as capitation fees or other taxable grants from local authorities.

The VAT registration position of a charity is of fundamental importance to its trading activities or indeed to whether it decides to trade at all. Some charities which trade on a large scale have set up separate limited companies to carry on those activities, there being substantial income tax advantages in so doing. But such trading companies, assuming their annual taxable turnover to be in excess of £10,000, must register as a 'taxable person', and as such must account and pay VAT to the Crown on the value added by the company in the course of its trading.

Other charities are so organised that their work is carried out by separate branches in various parts of the country, each branch operating as a self-contained, autonomous unit. Provided that a branch in these circumstances has complete control over its financial and other affairs and is completely free to apply its resources as it thinks fit to fulfil its charitable aims, it can be treated for VAT purposes as a separate entity. Registration, in these circumstances, is necessary only where an individual branch itself exceeds the statutory limit of taxable turnover.

Fund-raising activities are often carried on by private individuals or unincorporated associations. Provided that they accept full legal and financial responsibility for organising these activities and are free to donate the profit to any charity of their own choice, the resulting turnover is regarded as being attributable to the fund-raiser rather than the charity which benefits. Individuals or associations who operate in this way are, of course, themselves subject to the normal rules and will be required to register and to pay VAT on such proceeds if their total taxable turnover exceeds the statutory limit. HM Customs and Excise advise anybody who is thinking of embarking on fund-raising work in this way to consult, in their own interest, their local VAT office, whether or not they are already registered for VAT purposes. Charities, too, must consider their position carefully before they decide to utilise, encourage or set up such freelance activities. They need to be absolutely satisfied about the integrity, motivation, efficiency, business acumen and flair of the fund-raisers. Because such persons are legally independent, the charity has no real control either over the expenses, which may be considerable and which largely cannot be checked, or the methods adopted, nor any legal entitlement to the funds raised.

There are many sharks in the fund-raising sea, but even when a charity and a separate fund-raising set-up are in apparent sympathy, there are nevertheless very real dangers of friction between them. Disharmony between a responsible charity and enthusiastic but unrealistic fund-raisers can occur very easily. Organisers of charity functions and other activities, although working independently of the charity to which they intend to donate the profits, are entitled to advertise their intentions in this respect. They act, in this sense and in the eyes of the public, on behalf of the charity, and its good name is therefore at stake. Nothing is worse for a charity than, say, a celebrity concert which flops through poor organisation or lack of expertise, or a fund-raising event which is announced as being for the benefit of the charity and which in practice results in vast expense and miniscule profit.

There are also legal considerations. Before utilising the services of an independent person or group, a charity may wish to take legal advice about whether there is any conflict with its charter of incorporation or constitution, or any question of limitation of membership under the Companies Act if the organisation is formed for the purpose of carrying on any business with the object of acquisition of gain.

As we explained above, many activities of charities are regarded as not being pursued in the course of business and are thus outside the scope of VAT. It follows that such activities are not reckoned as taxable turnover and do not affect the registration position. Equally, it follows that when a charity is registered for VAT in respect of other activities, the 'non-business' aspects of its work are treated separately. It cannot, therefore, reclaim VAT charged on goods and services supplied to it for 'non-business' purposes (although the Goodman Committee concluded that it *should* be free to reclaim VAT on expenses in excess of £25 a year).

Reliefs

A number of taxable supplies, although within the broad definition of 'business', nevertheless carry a zero rate of VAT. These are listed in Sch. 4 to the Finance Act 1972 (as amended) and reproduced in Customs and Excise Notice No. 701. Zero-rated supplies count as taxable when determining whether turnover exceeds the statutory limit for VAT registration, but a registered person, while not having to charge output tax on such supplies to his customers, can recover as input tax any VAT he has been charged by his own suppliers.

All exports are zero-rated, and so are most kinds of food sold for consumption off the premises.

The zero-rating of some items was specifically designed to relieve charitable supplies. These include, under specified conditions, supplies of talking books, certain medical or surgical aids and appliances to disabled people, and donated medical equipment.

In the context of fund-raising, the significant relief is the zero-rating of the supply (sale) of donated goods by charities that are 'established primarily for the relief of distress'. This means either the relief of poverty, or making provision for the cure, or mitigation, or prevention of, or for the care of persons suffering from or subject to, any disease or infirmity or disability affecting human beings. This includes the care of women before, during and after childbirth.

This zero-rating allows such charities to sell donated goods, whether new or not, in charity gift shops, at fêtes, bazaars and jumble sales, without attracting additional VAT. If the goods have been donated from the stock-in-trade of a 'taxable person' (e.g. a gift from a local company registered for VAT) the relief only applies if the cost of the goods to him did not exceed £10.

Where the goods are not sold by the charity (e.g. when they are sold by an independent charity shop), the zero rate cannot apply unless the seller merely acts on behalf of the charity and receives only a commission for the sale. In these circumstances, if the seller is registered for VAT, it will be due only on the commission. The seller will charge VAT on the commission to the charity, which, if registered for VAT, can recover it as input tax. Similarly, a charity shop which is registered for VAT either on its own account or as part of a larger organisation, may sell other new or used goods on behalf of their owners on a commission basis. VAT is due from the shop on any such commission but not on the actual proceeds from the sale of the goods. The net effect is that the VAT paid on each transaction will be the same as if the principal had sold the goods direct. He is neither better nor worse off in real terms than if he had sold the goods himself, and there is no advantage over any other sellers. Of course, if neither the seller nor the charity exceed the statutory limit on turnover and are not therefore registered for VAT, these points are academic.

Other supplies made in the course of business are held to be 'exempt'. There is a list, in Sch. 5 to the Finance Act 1972 (as amended), of supplies that are 'exempt' from VAT. The list is reproduced in Customs and Excise Notice No. 701. Like zero-rated supplies they carry no output tax, but they differ in that they do not count as taxable turnover and there is no entitlement to recover input tax in respect of them.

The significant exemption for fund-raisers is that afforded to the proceeds of betting, gaming and lotteries (i.e. the stakes or takings less only the winnings or value of prizes). The exemption does not extend to games of skill, to admission charges, session or participation charges made under s. 14 of the Gaming Act 1968, subscriptions to any club, nor (since November 1975) to the takings from gaming machines, all of which are taxable.

These then are the broad guidelines which fund-raisers must take into account. We regret their complexity, but they must be faced and related to other considerations, such as your organisation's income tax position, and whether you need to employ outside help in raising funds. Often, the overriding preoccupation is to avoid VAT registration altogether, either by limiting the scope and extent of fund-raising or by hiving off certain activities to independent organisers, but we have tried to show that this may be counter-productive. Individual decisions must be guided by the particular circumstances which apply, and we can only urge careful thought, and recommend that you seek further advice if any doubt remains.

9. Trading

Trading poses special problems for charities and voluntary organisations. It involves them in a commercial world for which they are not necessarily well fitted. Their good reputation is at stake and it is therefore particularly important that their business practices are beyond reproach and that they should be wary of entrepreneurs who seek to exploit rather than assist their charitable purposes. When a member of the public buys goods from or 'in aid of' a named charity, he is in part making an emotional response to a deserving need, and expects, and is entitled to expect, that his money will not be swallowed up in excessive overheads and expenses, and that a worthwhile profit on the transaction will be used for the purposes of the charity, whose most precious stock-in-trade is goodwill.

Another important factor in charity trading is the need to avoid complaints of unfair competition. Charities commonly enjoy privileges not available to ordinary businesses: for example, voluntary labour, rent-free shop premises, donated merchandise, and a claim to the public's charitable sympathy; direct competition in such circumstances will plainly be unwelcome and charities must tread very carefully.

These are ethical considerations. There are also practical dangers in fund-raising by trade, principally that when operated on any scale – beyond, say, the charitable bazaar – the enterprise is subject to normal commercial hazards, and far from proving profitable, may actually result in a loss. It follows that fund-raisers should either limit their activities to circumstances in which they are certain to make a profit and are free of legal complications, or should approach the venture with due regard for its viability, and with proper business acumen and knowledge. They should be aware, for instance, that most goods are chargeable with value added tax and that trading resulting in a turnover above a prescribed limit may involve liability to register as a VAT trader (see Chapter 8). Similarly, that apart from certain prescribed exemptions, profits of trade are within the scope of income or corporation tax (see Chapter 7).

Trading by voluntary organisations takes many forms. Some of these are so familiar by now as not to require further explanation: for example, bazaars, sales of work, sales by mail order and sales of greetings cards. Organisations which trade on any scale normally form a separate limited company for the purpose. Indeed, some are obliged to do so because of restrictions imposed by their articles of association. As well as giving the ordinary benefits of limited liability, this allows the trading subsidiary to pass its profits to the parent charity under a deed of covenant, enabling the charity to reclaim corporation tax (see Chapter 7).

One of the most popular forms of trading by voluntary organisations is that carried on in 'charity shops'. Some description of their organisation will serve to illustrate most of the hurdles which are likely to be encountered when raising funds by way of trade.

Charity shops

The most important consideration in deciding whether to open a charity shop is its potential viability. Despite the proliferation of such shops in our towns and cities, and despite their increasing sophistication, the fact has to be faced that they demand a great deal in terms of time and effort and may require a considerable financial outlay in order to yield a small commercial profit. As such, they can be one of the more expensive forms of fund-raising. Against the potential takings must be set the expenses:

Rent

Rent is an important cost unless the shop is 'borrowed' during a temporary untenanted period. Such arrangements are sometimes available to local groups who, being on the spot, can observe the vacation of suitable premises and move quickly to negotiate with the owner or agent and, if successful, to stock and staff the shop. There are advantages to the owner who can thus be relieved of the burden of rates, and whose shop is less likely to suffer damage and deterioration if occupied.

Rates

Some measure of relief is afforded to charities. The General Rate Act 1967, s. 40, as amended by the Rating (Charity Shops) Act

1976, provides that if premises in England and Wales are occupied by a charity (or by trustees for a charity) and used wholly or mainly for charitable purposes then the rates on them shall not exceed one-half of the normal charge. Upon written application, rating authorities have discretion to fix the rate below 50 per cent, even to abate it altogether. The 1976 Act makes clear that charity shops qualify if used 'wholly or mainly for the sale of goods donated to a charity' and 'the proceeds of sale (after any deduction of expenses) are applied for the purposes of a charity'. Parallel provisions cover charity shops in Scotland – Local Government (Financial Provisions etc.) (Scotland) Act 1962, s. 4.

Corporation and value added taxes

The position here is of some complexity but is crucial. It is discussed in detail in Chapters 7 and 8, but the practical problem is to reconcile and make the most of a number of tax concessions.

In principle, the profits of charity-shop trading are liable to corporation tax. However, it is customary for the shop business to be operated by a separate trading company, which donates its profits to the charity under deed of covenant. Thus, as we have previously noticed, the tax deducted and paid over to the Inland Revenue by the trading company can be recouped by the charity.

Liability to value added tax depends on whether the trading entity is 'registered'. Registration can in some circumstances be obtained voluntarily, but is anyway mandatory where the 'taxable turnover' exceeds or is likely to exceed £10,000 per annum. Taxable turnover includes the proceeds of the sale of donated goods (gifts in kind), but such goods carry a zero rate of VAT *if donated to and sold by* a charity established primarily for the relief of *human* distress. When, to minimise the impact of corporation tax, trading is carried on by an independent trading company, it apparently follows that the goods are *not* sold by the charity and the zero rate cannot be applied. However, it is possible for the trading company to sell donated goods as the agent of the charity. Then the true seller is the charity, and the zero rate, if otherwise appropriate, may be applied (see Chapter 8). Since the sale of genuine gifts by charities does not, in practice, attract corporation tax, this arrangement should not prejudice the charity's tax position with the Inland Revenue.

In some cases, a charity shop may be run by an autonomous branch of a charity, when VAT registration and hence liability to VAT would apply only if the taxable turnover *of the branch* exceeded £10,000 per annum. Even then, donated goods as defined above would be zero-rated and genuine gifts would not normally attract corporation tax.

Other expenses

1. Remuneration of person in charge of shop. It may, of course, be possible to find a suitable volunteer to manage the shop. But to secure the services of the right person it may well be desirable to make some payment.
2. Expenses of voluntary helpers.
3. Administrative expenses. These include the till, accounting and security arrangements, and supervisory management.
4. Heating and lighting
5. Cost of new goods
6. Insurance. Insurance should be obtained to cover public liability, stock, and cash (wherever kept).

Practical considerations

Only when the sums are done, can an estimate of profit be forecast. It will then be a matter of judgement whether it is worth proceeding. If so, practical arrangements must be carefully considered. There are a number of golden rules here.

1. The shop must be located in a busy shopping area, ideally where a second-hand shop would not appear incongruous.
2. The person in charge must be competent, imaginative and honest.
3. To have any hope of making a worthwhile profit, the bulk of the merchandise must be donated. Rigorously select only the best articles. It is better to dispose of substandard goods as waste (see Chapter 11) – not only do they provide a poor financial profit, they make the shop look shabby and present the poorest possible image of the charity. Charity shops should definitely not be a kind of long-term jumble sale.
4. Price goods (especially collectors' items) realistically. Mark the price – failure to do so will put off many customers.
5. Display the goods in an attractive and orderly way.
6. Second-hand stock can be leavened with a modest quantity of new goods – craft ware from Third World developing countries is particularly suitable – thus widening the appeal of the shop. But the new goods may attract VAT and necessitate separate accounting.
7. Try to keep the shop open during normal shopping hours.

We hope that this has not been off-putting. In practice, many of the problems of operating charity shops (or any other form of trading) are matters of common sense, the bureaucratic hurdles are relatively easy to surmount, and if costs are kept down the financial rewards far outweigh the expenses. But it is well to be armed with the facts before starting.

Unsolicited goods

The Unsolicited Goods and Services Act 1971 aims to protect members of the public against 'inertia' selling – the supply of goods with a view to their acquisition without any prior request. A private individual receiving goods in these circumstances, having neither agreed to acquire them nor to return them, and having no reasonable cause to believe that they were sent for the purposes of a trade or business, may after six months from the date of receipt of the goods (during which time the sender is allowed to repossess) treat them as his own property and as if they had been an unconditional gift. All rights of the sender are then extinguished and the recipient is entitled to use, deal with or dispose of the goods as he sees fit. Alternatively, if, not less than 30 days before the end of the six-month period, the recipient gives the sender a written notice of the unsolicited receipt of the goods and an address at which they can be repossessed, he may after 30 days from the day on which the notice is given (during which time the sender is allowed to repossess them) similarly treat them as his own property. This notice may be sent by post.

To sum up, anyone who receives unsolicited goods may, after six months (or sooner if notice of unsolicited receipt is given) during which the sender has not been denied the opportunity to repossess them, treat them as his own. No payment whatsoever is required or enforceable.

It is an offence either to demand payment for unsolicited goods, or to assert 'a present or prospective right to payment'. Any invoice or similar document stating the amount of any payment, and not stating as prominently (or more prominently) that no claim is made to the payment, is regarded as asserting a right to the payment.

The implications of this legislation on charities who send unsolicited goods looking for payment in return are quite obvious. The best that they can hope for are voluntary donations in recognition of the goods received, but they run the very real risk that many people will be antagonised if they are approached in this way.

81

10. Sponsorship

Sponsored endeavour

At their best, sponsored activities rate as one of the most attractive ways of raising funds. The financial objectives are linked with, indeed stimulate, endeavour, and the whole proceeds, apart from very minor expenses, go to the promoting organisation. The events can capture the imagination and interest of sponsors and participants alike and their response is positive, involved and healthy. Apart from raising money, they increase people's awareness of the needs of the society to which they belong.

From every point of view, organisers should aim to promote exciting, attractive, eye-catching events which will gain the maximum publicity and attention. It is an area of fund-raising which calls for flair and imagination, for ideas and vision. By now, hundreds of sponsored events have been organised – we give some of them below – but there is no limit to the possibilities. One enthusiast walked around the coastline of Britain, while Norman Croucher, the intrepid climber on two artificial legs, scaled the Peruvian Andes.

Here are the basic rules.

1. Plan well in advance. Don't spoil a good idea by poor organisation, or by failing to capitalise on securing good sponsorship. Take warning from the true story of the boy who ran 126 laps of his local football ground (about 26 miles in all) and was then found to have been sponsored at 1½p a lap!

2. Leave no publicity stone unturned (see Chapter 12).

3. Try to promote an event in which the sponsorship promotes extraordinary effort to win the donation, and in which the sponsor can see that he will not be 'taken to the cleaners'. It is obvious that most people will be wary of sponsoring a known long-distance walker at so much per mile with an open-ended commitment. In this context, it might be better

to seek sponsorship on a per-mile basis for, say, ten miles (which everyone can be expected to do), on a per-two-mile basis for the next ten miles, on a per-three-mile basis for the next nine miles, and so on. We dislike the idea of placing a fixed upper limit on contributions. This restricts both the generosity of the sponsor and the effort of the participant.

Safety in sponsored walks

Avoid exposing participants to unnecessary or excessive risks. Don't plan a walk along busy public roads or demand efforts which go beyond the extraordinary into the superhuman category. Safety first! Our advice in respect of sponsored walks would be to avoid public roads altogether. Keep to commons, parks or open country-side. But if this is not possible, then be sure that you check your plans with the police, and seek their advice.

Country walks need careful planning. Advice is given in the *Country Code*, available from the Countryside Commission, John Dower House, Crescent Place, Cheltenham, Gloucestershire GL50 3RA. A particularly imaginative route, used by the Save the Children Fund in April 1978, is the London Countryway – a continuous 205-mile route encircling London, and passing through superb countryside. It is described in *A Guide to the London Countryway* (London: Constable, 1978) by Keith Chesterton, who conceived and planned the route over a period of six years.

The Department of the Environment publish an attractive leaflet, *Safety and Sponsored Walks*, available free from Directorate of Information, DOE, 2 Marsham Street, London SW1P 3EB.

The following checklist of safety precautions on sponsored walks is reproduced by permission of the Royal Society for the Prevention of Accidents.

1. A minimum age of at least 16 years is preferable.
2. Where younger persons are included they should be adequately supervised by responsible adults.
3. Suitable walking footwear should be worn.
4. If night walking is involved light-coloured clothing, visible to drivers, should be worn with, if possible, reflective armbands.
5. The police should be asked for their advice on choice of route, time and day and their directions should be obeyed.
6. In any event, heavily trafficked roads should be avoided, especially at night.

7. Walkers should be started at intervals, mass starts are dangerous.
8. The start and finish should be off the road.
9. Participants should be reminded of the requirements on pages 4–6, and on page 46, of the Highway Code.
10. They should be instructed, where there is no footpath, to walk on the right-hand side of the road facing oncoming traffic.
11. Any vehicles used in a supervisory capacity should not travel at a slow speed and thus cause obstruction to other traffic.
12. If a gate has to be opened make sure that it is shut again, so that cattle cannot stray on to the highway.
13. There should be a follow-up system to ensure that no participant remains behind requiring help.

Some ideas for sponsored activities

Abstinence	Jogs	Singing marathons
Bridge-crossing	Knitting	Skate-boarding
Chess marathons	Litter removal	Slimming
Clearing land	Non-smoking	Sunflower growing
Climbing	Ploughing	Swimming
Darts	Pub-crawling	Table tennis
Decorating	Reading marathons	Walks
Expeditions	Scrabble marathons	Water-skiing
Gardening	Silence	

One of our favourites is the sponsored jog, and an explanation of its organisation will serve as a guide to the important features in any other form of sponsored activity.

Volunteers undertake to jog around a local circuit, having previously secured sponsorship at so much per lap from as many people as possible. From a publicity point of view it is obviously an advantage if the jog can be held at a football, cricket or other sports ground, preferably for several hours before a sporting event which the public will attend in large numbers. The local football club manager, for instance, if properly approached, might agree to a jog preceding the Saturday game, and to the joggers staying on to see the match free of the usual admission charge. This will certainly help with the recruitment of young joggers. But if this or similar arrangements are not possible, a jog can nevertheless be successfully held round any suitable field.

Joggers can be of any age, but our experience points to the age group 11–14 as offering the best prospects of success. Schoolchildren in this age range are not too involved with examinations and their boundless physical energy combines with a genuine will to help.

Organisation of the jog should begin about eight weeks before the intended date and should follow the following basic pattern.

1. Fix the date, time and place, securing the necessary permissions. Avoid dates when school holidays preclude prior contact with local schools. Remember that a football club manager will have to put a request to use his ground before his board. Write on headed notepaper and explain the reasons for which the money is to be raised.

2. Produce, say, 150 copies of the jog sponsorship forms (see Figure 10.1).

3. Seek the cooperation of headmasters of local schools, by asking their consent to address morning assembly. These contacts are best made by telephone and personal interview: written requests tend to be more easily resisted or ignored.

4. Arrange for your best speaker(s) to address the schools' morning assemblies. The speech should be short and to the point, but rousing, leading to a call for volunteers. Sponsorship forms should be issued to volunteers: school staff may arrange this and subsequent collection. In any event, the arrangements should be clearly stated on a sheet with the sponsorship form (see Figure 10.2). Volunteers can similarly be raised from local youth organisations, from branch members and friends. The number of volunteers must, of course, be limited to a total which can be reasonably accommodated and controlled at the chosen venue.

5. On the day of the jog it will be necessary to have one person as jog marshal, and one jog teller to endorse the forms with the number of laps completed. As the joggers complete each lap, they collect a small piece of card, or a ticket, from the marshal. At the completion of their jog they hand their tickets and jog forms to the jog teller who endorses the number of laps completed accordingly.

6. Remember to take some form of refreshment to spur the joggers to their best endeavours; it may also be thought appropriate to award some token of gratitude – say a badge.

7. Make sure that the joggers know the arrangements for handing in the money collected from their sponsors.

8. Try to get a local celebrity to lead off the jog.

(Name of organisation)
SPONSORED JOG
(Venue, date, and times)

Name of jogger _____	School (*if appropriate*)_____
Address _____	_____
_____	_____

The person named above is taking part in a sponsored jog to raise money for ——
We hope that you will give both the cause and those taking part your encouragement by giving as much as possible for each lap completed. Sponsors are requested to fill in their name and address below, promising a certain amount of money per lap to the jogger. One lap is about —— yards. After the jog, the certificate below will be completed so you will know how many laps your jogger managed.

Signed _____ (Jog Organiser)
Name and address _____

This is to certify that _____ Completed —— laps
_____ Signed _____ (Jog Teller)

I pledge to sponsor the person named above at the sum per lap shown below

Name	Address	Amount per lap		Total
		First 20 laps	Subsequent laps	

Figure 10.1 Specimen form for recording sponsors of a sponsored jog

INFORMATION FOR JOGGERS
FOREWORD
(An explanation of the purpose of the jog)
BEFORE THE EVENT
1. Try to get as many sponsors as possible at so much per lap on the attached sponsor form.
2. Bring it with you to the jog, where the jog teller will certify how many laps you complete.
3. Make sure your name, address and school (if any) are clearly shown on your sponsor form.

AT THE JOG
1. Joggers are asked to make their own way to ——.
2. —— will be there at —— to lead off the jog.
3. You can start at —— or later if you prefer.
4. Joggers should use entrance —— and report to ——.
5. Please wear sensible shoes, preferably gym shoes.
6. Jogging will be in a clockwise direction.
7. At the completion of each lap, you will be given a token by the jog teller.
8. When you have finished jogging, please present the tokens to the jog teller, who will certify the amount of laps completed. This is VERY IMPORTANT, because failure to do so will disqualify the jogger from the right to collect in money from the sponsors.
9. Participation in the jog entitles joggers to *(e.g. stay behind to watch the game free of charge)*.

AFTER THE EVENT
1. Please collect the money promptly so that it can be used to help the cause as soon as possible.
2. The form and money should be returned to ——.
3. Congratulations and thank you.

Figure 10.2 Specimen information sheet for sponsored joggers

Commercial sponsorship

Sponsorship of significant events and projects by large companies is common. There is mutual benefit. The charity has the certainty of a firm financial base, while the sponsor enjoys some first-class publicity.

Winning support is largely a matter of the right approach, personal initiative and/or having influential contacts, and we deal with this aspect in some depth in Chapter 13.

The outstanding example of commercial sponsorship is, of course, the support given to sport which, in recent years, has extended to many important events. The reason for this particular beneficence is not hard to find: sport attracts vast audiences as well as press, radio and television coverage and thus the name of the sponsor is carried into innumerable households. Voluntary organisations cannot offer this kind of publicity but the basic principle of mutual benefit holds good, albeit on a smaller scale. This is particularly true of the local scene. Companies may well be attracted to proposals to have their name associated with significant events which attract and interest the public in considerable numbers. Organisations engaged in artistic and theatrical activities have found this to be true and there are many other kinds of public events which could similarly benefit from commercial sponsorship.

The support may not be exclusively financial. Some big companies will be prepared to help with the organisation of special events and are often well fitted, both in terms of manpower and equipment, to do so. The essential caution in this situation is that the voluntary body and sponsor company should liaise effectively so that there is perfect understanding about the division of practical organisational responsibilities.

We should not like to leave the impression that all commercial sponsorship is motivated by self-interest. A great deal of support is given behind the scenes in a quiet way. Many trading companies prefer to be associated with a special project or event (especially if it has a ready correlation with their own business interests) rather than lend their assistance to the wider aims of a charitable cause.

Long-term sponsorship

Even more valuable and selfless is the system of long-term sponsorship to meet particular needs, in which the sponsor can identify his giving with specific results and can become personally involved at a deeper level than merely contributing money. An example is the scheme run by the Save the Children Fund, aimed at gaining support to provide deprived children in more than 20 countries with an education on which to build their future. For £50 a year, people in Britain and the Commonwealth can sponsor an individual child. If the subscription is covenanted (see Chapter 7) its value is enhanced by about half as much again. Each sponsor is given the personal story of the child his money supports, a photograph and an address for correspondence, and is kept informed of the child's progress and changing circumstances. Sometimes a close relationship grows between sponsor and child and often children write to their sponsors telling them in their own words how their life is developing and of their hopes for the future.

Another particularly interesting sponsorship scheme is run by Voluntary Service Overseas (VSO), which sends medical, agricultural, educational and technical volunteers for at least two years to Third World countries. VSO invites sponsors, be they individuals or companies, to sponsor a volunteer for a year at £300. The sponsor is encouraged to keep in personal touch with the volunteer and to follow his or her progress in what is often a very exciting project. Most volunteers are only too glad to write to their sponsors regularly, reporting on their work. In the case of a company, the work of a volunteer can provide particularly interesting news for the company magazine, where all employees can share in following the volunteer's progress.

Most people like to feel that the money they donate is being used for something tangible and not being swallowed up in a general fund. Sponsorship schemes offer just such a positive coalescence of gift and result. They are a powerful inducement to philanthropy.

11. Waste collection

Many local groups have found that there is a market for certain types of waste materials: paper, scrap metals and textiles come readily to mind. With the cooperation of the public and a team of enthusiastic collectors, really substantial quantities of materials can be salvaged which might otherwise be totally wasted. These collections not only provide funds for local causes, they make a positive contribution to the nation's anti-waste programme, conserving valuable raw materials and reducing our import bill. So important is the conservation aspect that the Departments of Industry and of the Environment have jointly sponsored a national drive to save and recycle waste materials. The 'National Anti-Waste Programme' publishes an excellent booklet, *Save and Recycle: A Guide to Voluntary Waste Collection*, which is accompanied by a list of waste merchants for your particular locality. It is available free from Freepost, NAWP, Ashdown House, 123 Victoria Street, London SW1E 6RB (no stamp is needed on your letter). We are greatly indebted to the Secretariat of the Programme for permission to make use of its informative literature throughout this chapter.

The official guide gives a great deal of helpful advice both generally and concerning the collection of specific materials, and is indispensable to those who seriously intend to go ahead with a definite scheme. In bringing out some of the more significant points we hope that we may assist those who are uncertain about where to start or whether to start at all.

Many waste merchants are keen to receive supplies and therefore to encourage voluntary collection schemes, but there are, as usual, a number of general rules.

1. When you sell waste materials you are trading, and the normal business principles and trading risks apply. You will wish to seek out a fair deal and a helpful buyer. Waste merchants are, of course, middlemen and aim to make a

profit – sometimes a substantial one. Wherever and whenever possible it makes more sense to sell direct to an industrial user of waste materials. Remember that the market in waste materials tends to be unstable. Make sure there is a demand for a particular material *before* you collect it. Be guided by your buyer. Find out exactly and keep under review what is required, to what extent the material needs to be sorted or graded and, of course, whether the best price on offer justifies the cost and work involved.

2. Plan your arrangements for collection, transport and storage. Bulky materials can present problems, and your arrangements need to be adequate.

3. Inform your local authority about what you intend to do. Your activities should complement, not conflict with, the statutory services. Given a polite approach, your local authority may well be able to help or to offer advice.

4. Secure and retain the goodwill of contributors by explaining the scheme properly, collecting regularly, and letting people know the results achieved.

5. Keep in close touch with your outlets. Be prepared to follow market trends. A guide to price fluctuations specially prepared for voluntary collectors, is now available. This can be obtained from *Materials Reclamation Weekly,* PO Box NG 109, Davis House, 69/77 High Street, Croydon, Surrey CR9 1QH, and, strange as it may seem, appears on the first Saturday of every *month*.

6. Ensure that your activities are properly insured. It would be prudent to offer your voluntary helpers some cover against personal accident, and it is essential that vehicles used to transport goods are insured for that purpose. You will doubtless wish to insure any premises, stock or machinery against the usual risks. Some local groups operate as branches of larger or national organisations and may be covered by centralised insurance arrangements. If not, the best advice is to consult a broker or insurance company (or more than one) and explain the scope of your intended operations. You will then get expert guidance.

7. If your collections are on a random door-to-door basis you may need a licence under the house-to-house collections legislation. Check with your licensing authority (see Chapter 2 for details).

8. Your activities may be affected by other legislation, e.g.

Building Regulations (check with your local authority), Health and Safety at Work etc. Act 1974 (check with the nearest office of the Health and Safety Executive) or fire regulations (check with your local Chief Fire Officer).

9. If you intend to use a heavy goods vehicle, the driver must, of course, hold an HGV licence.

Paper

Paper is top of the pops among voluntary collectors, partly because it is easy to collect and transport and partly because most households, offices and shops have waste paper in abundance. In the recent past, demand for waste paper has fallen off, but, with government encouragement, the long-term prospects are good. Some local authorities operate fairly comprehensive paper-collecting schemes, but most do not; this is therefore an area where prior consultation is highly desirable. There are, of course, a variety of grades of paper, and the demand pattern is particularly inconsistent in this trade. It is important to be guided by your waste-paper merchant. The paper must be stored clean and dry, and needs to be secured in tight bundles.

Scrap metal

Scrap metal is divided into two basic types: 'ferrous' (wholly or mainly iron) and 'non-ferrous' (other metals, e.g. aluminium, lead, copper, zinc). The ferrous metals are attracted by a magnet, whereas other metals (apart from nickel-rich stainless steel) are not. The non-ferrous metals are considerably more valuable and it is worth while separating these out.

The collection of metals presents difficult problems. Many household items are bulky and, since they do not become obsolete on a regular basis, it is impracticable to organise collections in a systematic way. The most common form of waste metal – 'tin' cans – occupy a great amount of space relative to their weight, are usually discarded complete with the nasty remnants of the contents, and are generally made largely of steel, offering a poor monetary return. More popular items – tin foil and aluminium ring pulls – again yield rather poor proceeds. The official estimate is 10p for 5000 milk bottle tops or 200 rings. But if you are able to organise a large number of young collectors, with spare time on their hands, the quantities collected can make this a worthwhile enterprise. Old lead piping, and discarded aluminium and copper items are more valuable, but finding them may be difficult. Householders are well aware that they fetch a high price and, in practice, sell such items direct to local scrap merchants.

Textiles

Textiles can be sold through various outlets – wearable clothing through jumble sales and charity shops, waste for reclamation or use as wiping cloths. A better price can be obtained if you are able to do some sorting of the waste into the various synthetic and natural fibres and also by colour. It is also conspicuously true that you will get a better deal from users than from rag merchants. But users need waste of specific kinds in quantity and regularly. Some charities – for example Oxfam and the Spastics Society – are well organised in this respect, and it is probable that they will offer better terms for your waste than a commercial dealer. Oxfam have a waste reclamation depot in Huddersfield: write for details to Oxfam Wastesaver, 274 Banbury Road, Oxford OX2 7DZ; telephone Oxford 56777. The Spastics Society's depot is at 16 Bridge Road East, Welwyn Garden City, Hertfordshire.

Oil

Motor vehicle sump oil is currently wasted in vast quantities. It is estimated that motorists changing their own oil throw away over 30,000 tonnes a year, and many of them have some difficulty in getting rid of it. Even allowing for the fact that some local authorities and garages will accept waste oil, there is considerable scope for voluntary organisations. The Chemical Recovery Association, Petrol House, Hepscott Road, London E9 8HD, has produced a free guide which gives information on setting up and running an 'oil collection centre' (including the relevant safety regulations). If large quantities of oil are collected (upwards of six 45-gallon drums) dealers who belong to the above association will collect it free of charge. In setting up a collection centre, a suitable site is necessary, and prior liaison with the local authority is essential.

Glass

Glass waste (cullet) is needed in increasing quantities for recycling in a variety of products. There should be no difficulty in finding sources of waste glass, but it may be less easy to locate a buyer. To be acceptable, the cullet must usually be sorted by colour – basically clear, amber, and green – *and apart from labels must contain nothing other than glass*. Small amounts of window

93

glass can be included with clear bottle glass, but mirrors, light bulbs and other types of glass should be avoided. The main problem is that waste glass is normally required in very large quantities which are heavy, bulky and risky to handle and transport, and this may be beyond the scope of many voluntary collectors. The official guide draws attention to the Recycling Advisory Bureau, Glass Manufacturers Federation, 19 Portland Place, London W1N 4BH, and we strongly encourage those who may be thinking of collecting glass to seek full advice before taking any practical steps.

Publicity

Whatever you decide to collect, the official guide gives much useful information on publicising your scheme. It is clearly essential to let people know precisely what you want, how you want it, and how you will collect it. As with other forms of fund-raising, people need to be told on whose behalf the collections are being made, and where the proceeds will go. The publicity must also have *impact*, and to this end the National Anti-Waste Programme has produced a really good poster which prominently features the impressive campaign symbol but leaves ample space for overprinting. A copy is included with the official 'Save and Recycle' guide, and further supplies are available from the NAWP at Ashdown House, 123 Victoria Street, London SW1E 6RB. The guide also gives artwork ideas for overprinting and for the production of additional leaflets or handbills.

Taxes

As trading operations, the proceeds of waste collections are potentially liable to both income (or corporation) tax and value added tax, but given certain conditions neither may bite in practice. A fuller explanation is given in Chapters 7 and 8.

12. Publicity

Success in fund-raising depends to a considerable extent on adequate and effective publicity. It is the means by which the public you hope to interest is made aware of the needs and the work of your organisation. All forward-looking national organisations are well aware of this and rely heavily upon the services of professional employees or associates in the areas of press and public relations, advertising and print design. Apart from some advice on press conferences, this chapter is directed towards local groups and branches of charities who lack professional assistance in this field.

Many local organisations find it worth while to appoint a publicity officer, with special responsibility for liaison with the media. This arrangement has distinct advantages: it allows the person most gifted in this way to use his or her talents to the best advantage, and it establishes a specific personal link between the organisation and local radio and newspapers. Instead of being an extra job for an already hard-pressed chairman or secretary, it is tackled with enthusiasm and the publicity officer rapidly gains contacts, specialist knowledge and expertise.

Local press

'News is something which, because of its variation from the normal, compels attention.' This axiom needs always to be borne in mind when submitting stories to the local press. Fascinating though you may find your own coffee mornings or jumble sales, you have to remember that there are hundreds of such events even in a small locality during the course of a year. Therefore, however worthy you think your particular event may be, unless it has an interesting news angle, the local press is unlikely to give you free publicity in its editorial columns. It is a serious mistake to attempt to exaggerate the importance of an event and/or engineer misleading publicity in an attempt to encourage the local reporter to come along. For if when he arrives he finds that there is really nothing of particular interest to his readers, he will be wary of responding to such ploys in the future.

However, local newspapers exist to publish local news and thrive on good stories. They will always welcome items which are *genuinely* newsworthy and interesting. The message therefore, is to avoid bombarding the paper with trivial copy at frequent intervals. Seek publicity only when you have something which the newspaper is likely to consider will be of interest to its readers. In this way one may build up a mutual trust and respect between the organisation and the newspaper, each relying upon the other.

Try to get to know your local reporter and editor personally. If the aims and objectives of your organisation are explained in a friendly chat, they are likely to be more sympathetic to the material you send them, and they may well be prepared to give you guidance on the sort of information they require and the style in which they prefer it to be presented.

Sometimes you will wish to announce an event through the means of a *press release*. This is often the most convenient form of providing hard facts in outline. A newspaper editor has an enormous amount to read and therefore he welcomes material which is presented in such a way that he can establish the facts at a glance. A compelling headline will help to grab his attention. 'Biggest tortoise in the world leads sponsored walk' might provoke him to read on, and decide to follow the story up. The body of the release should be clear, short and to the point, preferably on one page using double-spacing. It must contain the name of a person to contact and a day and evening telephone number, and ideally should be followed up by a telephone call to establish a personal contact. All reporters do most of their business by telephone, and rely on rapid contact. If they cannot reach you by telephone, they are unlikely to write.

A reporter is a very busy person. If he comes to your event at all, he is liable to have to pop in and out rather quickly. It is vital that he is properly met by someone who is fully primed with all the facts which he will need: the aims of the organisation, how much money it is hoped to raise, names and status of officers, important visitors and speakers and background notes. If photographs are required, you should be well aware in advance of who should be included in these pictures, and you must be able to identify clearly the people involved. It is all too easy, during a convivial evening, to neglect these simple points. Remember that although you are involved in the event, the reporter is unlikely to be so committed and merely wants to do a serious job of work and complete his assignment as speedily and effectively as possible.

If you have to rely on giving your own account of an event after it has taken place, remember the golden rule: newspapers want stories with human interest or an unorthodox slant. But don't try to produce a 'paper-ready' article yourself. Stick to the facts. Every paper has its own style and it is inevitable that its staff writers will refurbish what you have submitted to suit the image of the newspaper, to exclude waffle, and to keep the piece down to the limits of the available space.

Remember, too, that each edition of a paper is normally 'put to bed' (i.e. completed and ready for printing) some time before it appears in the shops. Submit your copy in good time to meet the appropriate editorial deadline, not only for the obvious practical reasons, but also because greater consideration is likely to be given to your story at times other than the last-minute rush. Again, don't fail to give a daytime and evening telephone number.

Local radio

This is a rapidly expanding and popular form of communication. Both BBC and independent radio stations are becoming increasingly sensitive to the continuing involvement of the local community in the production of their programmes, and are therefore more than ever before responsive to ideas and suggestions of content. Programme makers are particularly alive to the value of immediacy in the presentation of local events and of the impact created by involving local people in their presentations. Most local radio stations would echo the BBC's belief that 'local radio should be not only to, for and about the community but *by* it as well'.

The BBC now has 20 local stations, and independent local radio 19. This is only a beginning, and it is clear that the development of local broadcasting has a very healthy future, serving local populations throughout the country. Even more than the press, local radio stations, with an average output of 10 hours a day, are hungry for local information and ideas. Since they set out to serve their neighbourhood, they are certain to be receptive to organisations which seek to benefit the local community. Moreover, particularly in the case of the smaller stations, they work on a restricted budget with a limited staff and cannot do without the active participation of members of the public.

At present, local radio's potential for advancing charitable work seems to us to be under-utilised. Much that we have said about the approach to newspapers applies with equal force to the radio networks, but here there is even greater scope for one's message to be presented effectively. There are opportunities for the presentation of news (e.g. advance notice of events), interviews and features, and it should not be difficult to interest the local station in any of these provided that you have worked out a firm, well-planned idea of what you wish to present. You should be aiming to *provide* a basis for really interesting locally oriented material rather than seeking a supportive service from the professionals.

There are many ways of making radio broadcasting lively and compelling. Good scripting is one of these, with an eye to an opening which grabs the listeners' attention and a finish which points the way ahead. Good speakers are, of course, essential: a well-known personality or celebrity may be able to help, but remember that the qualification here is not status, but the ability to put the message over in an interesting and convincing way with a voice which is warm and alive. The chairman of your organisation may not be the best man for this job. Remember, too, that many ordinary people among your membership have fascinating stories to tell: real-life experience is a good deal more dramatic than a cold presentation of facts. Interviews are always interesting and if used for a feature programme can be pre-recorded. On any given subject it is possible to canvass views from a wide range of people: the local MP, experts, religious leaders, members and the man in the street. Finally, local sound effects, say the noise of a street market, can bring colour and life to the broadcast and compel attention. Such material may be as manna to the local radio producer, always on the lookout for lively, contemporary, relevant programmes.

A radio interview should be seen as an opportunity rather than an ordeal. It is important to be as natural as possible. Interviews should sound spontaneous, so written notes are not desirable unless they are used simply to remind you of a title or figures you might otherwise forget. Local radio aims to sound like someone talking to his next-door neighbour, and interviewers are usually marvellously relaxed people. A good interviewer will have a chat before the serious business of interviewing begins in order to draw out the main points, so be prepared to brief him quickly with, say, three appropriate aspects of your subject so that he knows the broad lines on which to conduct his interview. The questions are likely to be open-ended and will ask 'where?', 'what?', 'why?', 'how much?', because straight yes and no answers make uninteresting broadcasting. In some cases voice training for spokesmen and officials of local organisations is provided, to help them express themselves to their audience in what may be an unfamiliar medium. The BBC makes the comment that some people are natural broadcasters, but for those who aren't, advice and training can work wonders. Don't be afraid to ask for help in producing and scripting messages and stories.

It is possible that the interview will be conducted at a location away from the studios, perhaps in someone's home. In such places, extraneous noises which pass unnoticed in ordinary life are picked up and spoil radio transmissions. Make sure that a really quiet room is available, free from interruptions and 'noises off'.

It is worth remembering that every BBC local radio station has an education officer. For those whose fund-raising projects have an educational content, e.g. to draw attention to the plight of neglected old people in the context of their local social environment, the education officer may be the most suitable initial point of contact, though 'education' is interpreted differently in different areas. Otherwise, one can contact the news editor, head of features, programmes organiser or even the station manager. It is obviously better if approaches can be made on a personal and friendly basis and to this end it is well worth while to have developed knowledge of the kind of programmes which are normally put out and to have established friendly links with those directly responsible for the production or presentation of the programmes that are suitable to your purpose. This can be done in a number of ways. Local radio staff are usually very pleased to meet requests to go round the station and watch programmes being made. This hospitality can be reciprocated by inviting a member of the station staff to talk to the organisation about the work and role of local broadcasting.

Be sure to put your ideas on paper as well as by telephone and cover all the relevant facts. Be ready to answer queries and to provide further information. The locations of regional radio stations may be less well known than those of newspapers and a list of those which are currently on the air is provided in the appendix at the back of the book.

For further reading a booklet, *Serving Neighbourhood and Nation*, is available from BBC, 35 Marylebone High Street, London W1M 4AA; and *ILR: Independent Local Radio* is available free from Independent Broadcasting Authority, 70 Brompton Road, London SW3.

Other local publicity material

It is our experience that local organisations can benefit greatly by the use of posters and leaflets, and by the regular issue of a newsletter or magazine, quite apart from any material which may be received from a national headquarters. There are usually talented people about who can produce any necessary artwork, or it may stimulate even greater interest if a competition is organised for, say, a poster design.

Leaflets are particularly valuable in informing local people about an organisation and bringing its needs to their notice. As an example, we illustrate in Figure 12.1 a simple leaflet (cover and two inside pages) which we designed for our local branch of the Multiple Sclerosis Society.

Press conferences

A press conference is a considerable undertaking and should be considered only when the information you wish to convey is sufficiently interesting and significant that it will be sure to stimulate the attention of those in the media business – in other words, when you are able to provide your guests with information or a story which will be of general interest to their listeners, viewers or readers. The launching of a major fund-raising campaign would certainly be such an occasion.

Preparation and research

Having decided to call a conference, the organiser's commitment must be enthusiastic and thorough. He must completely familiarise himself with the subject so that he can deal with any questions which may arise positively and authoritatively. If the subject is a fund-raising campaign, he will need to know all the financial details, must be prepared to deal with the press by telephone and be able to give relevant facts in response to enquiries: exactly how the money is to be spent, how much is needed (target), and when it should be achieved. The *Financial Times* will not be impressed if the organiser cannot quote the annual income and expenditure of the organisation!

Date

The date of the conference is important. As far as possible, it is obviously desirable to avoid conflicts with other major events. If you can find a time when news is a bit thin on the ground, you will

THE
MULTIPLE SCLEROSIS
SOCIETY
OF
GREAT BRITAIN
AND NORTHERN IRELAND

Headquarters:
4 Tachbrook Street, London SW1 V 1SJ

Royal Patron:
H.R.H. Princess Alice Duchess of Gloucester,
G.C.B., C.I., G.C.V.O., G.B.E.

President:
Angela, Countess of Limerick, G.B.E., C.H.

WALTHAM FOREST
BRANCH

President:
Cllr. Mrs. P. Williams, J.P.

Chairman:
Mr. L. R. Brown, 39 Courtland Avenue,
London E4 6DU.

Secretary:
Mr. H. G. Elliott, 104 The Ridgeway,
London E4 6PU.

Treasurer:
Miss E. M. Cook, 2 Forest Court, Forest Side,
London E4 6BJ.

The Branch is run by a small committee of unpaid,
voluntary workers—ordinary members of the public.

It relies entirely on voluntary contributions of time and
money. Administrative costs are minimal.

*Figure 12.1 Three pages from a publicity leaflet for a local branch of
the Multiple Sclerosis Society*

MULTIPLE SCLEROSIS is a common disease of the central nervous system which affects balance, vision, muscular co-ordination, and it can cause partial or even total paralysis. It can attack people of all ages.

WHAT DOES YOUR LOCAL BRANCH DO?

Assists members to secure necessary medical aids and other welfare needs.

Arranges suitable holidays for disabled members, providing or securing financial assistance where necessary.

Seeks to bring comfort to members by personal visits to home or hospital.

Organises regular club nights, with entertainment and social activities, occasional outings and other social events.

Raises funds for medical research into the causes and cure of Multiple Sclerosis and for extraordinary welfare need of members. (In 1975, the sum of £3,000 was put to the Society's research programme).

Liaises with, and makes representations to the Local Authority and other bodies on behalf of members in their day to day problems.

Arranges transport, where necessary, to ensure that members can take part in the various activities of the Branch.

Disseminates information on all aspects of Multiple Sclerosis and circulates a monthly Newsletter to all members.

We do not claim to be perfect, but we try. The degree to which we are successful largely depends on support we are able to attract. We need more help. If you are able to assist in any of the above activities, especially visiting, please contact the Secretary.

Figure 12.1 (cont'd)

I wish to become a Member of the Multiple Sclerosis Society.
I have Multiple Sclerosis.

Name .... MR.
                                                     MRS.
                                                     MISS
Address ....

....

....

Date ....

Please find enclosed cheque/P.O. £
my first annual subscription.

I wish to become an Associate Member of the Multiple Sclerosis Society and would be prepared to: —

Give a gift or make a donation
Display a poster
Take a collection box
Sell raffle tickets
Help by providing transport
Visit Members in their homes
Assist with fund raising
Hold a party in my garden.

Name .... MR.
                                                     MRS.
                                                     MISS
Address ....

....

....

Date ....

I enclose cheque/P.O. £   as my first
annual subscription.
I enclose cheque/P.O. as a donation.

NOTE

A Member is any person who has Multiple Sclerosis and wishes to belong to the Branch.

An Associate Member is any person willing to assist in any way.

Minimum subscription, 25p.

Figure 12.1 (cont'd)

plainly stand more chance of attracting a wide coverage. Bear in mind the publishing dates of the papers you wish to attract. If you are hoping to interest weekly and monthly periodicals, allow sufficient time before the publication dates for a piece to be made ready. If you want coverage in the Sunday papers, don't call the conference for a Monday (the traditional rest day). Choose a date sufficiently far ahead to allow reasonable notice to be given.

Whom to invite

This is not always as obvious as it may seem, for in addition to national and/or local press (listed in *Willing's Press Guide* or *Benn's Press Directory*), radio and television, there are innumerable specialist journals whose attention is relatively easier to attract and whose coverage is likely to be more comprehensive. Obviously, if you have a known contact on a particular paper you would invite him. Otherwise send your invitation to the editor or the news editor, or, if the subject of the conference has a specialist angle, such as motoring or gardening, the invitation should be sent to the correspondent who is known to cover this aspect. At the local level, do not neglect the parish magazine and all the other club magazines. Editors of these publications are always looking for news and you may be able to provide them with a good story and their readers with an interesting activity, that of raising funds for your good cause and becoming involved in your work.

The invitation

This should be accompanied by a press release. It is important to keep this short, giving only the hard facts and getting the essential message across in the first paragraph. It is worth spending time over the release. The primary requisite is that there should be a good story line which will command the interest of the press and provide a special reason for attending. It is usual to prepare a press kit providing back-up information, leaflets, annual report and, possibly, photographs. Part of this, e.g. the text of the conference speech (embargoed for use till the day), may be sent with the press release, but it is customary to issue the main kit at the conference itself, posting it to anyone who has not been able to turn up in person.

Follow-up

The invitation and press release should invariably be followed up by a telephone call. This has three objectives: to confirm, to inform and, above all, to persuade. One of the possibilities is that the invitation has been lost between offices or has gone to the wrong person. If you didn't write to a named individual, speak to the news desk, since any events which the paper has considered worth covering will have been logged in a diary in that office. You can ascertain whether your conference has been recorded, in which case, provided that no more important event occurs at the last minute, the chances are that a reporter will be detailed to come along. If there is no record in the diary, all is not lost. A tactful offer to send further information should be made. The organiser will need to be on his mettle, to have facts at his fingertips and to be positive and persuasive.

It is also a good idea to ask for the conference to be announced in the *UK Press Gazette* (Cliffords Inn, Fetter Lane, London EC4A 1PJ), a weekly paper taken by journalists which includes a list of newsworthy conferences and events for the forthcoming week. Subject to space being available, short entries (average length is about 14 words), are accepted free of charge. For example:

Friday, 12.45, unveiling of commemorative plaque by Lady Lustre, New Wing, Children's Hospital, Westminster. (Contact's name and telephone number.)

At the conference

Ensure that arrangements are satisfactory for visitors to find the conference room (and cloakroom) and for any disabled guests to be properly received and escorted. It is important to station a receptionist at the entrance of the conference room to give out press kits, answer queries, and to list those who attend for future reference or any necessary follow-up. This is one of the ways in which the names of relevant press contacts can be built up. It is helpful to issue identifying badges, but this cannot be done in advance; the people who attend will not necessarily be those who were invited. Make sure that visitors are welcomed and made to feel at home in the period before the formal presentation. Obviously, speeches should be interesting and brief, to allow time for questions. Experienced journalists will take notes, but ensure that the press kit contains the salient details: the correct spelling of the names of those involved, of the organisation and any other vital facts and statistics. The reporter will need to refer to these when he is back at his desk, and may also file the information for use on another occasion, establishing you as a positive link in that particular field of interest.

There must, of course, be scope for photographs to be taken, and suitable subjects should be primed and ready in advance: have in mind the sort of pictures you want to be taken. In case no press photographer turns up, the organisation should arrange one on its own initiative, so that suitable pictures can be sent to newspapers to enhance the story. Specialist papers and journals in particular often welcome such help.

Last but not least come the refreshments and the general chat which can be so useful in creating goodwill and winning the ear of individual reporters through personal conversation.

13. Special appeals

Advertising appeals

Throughout this guide we have been at pains to encourage 'do-it-yourself' fund-raising. In the matter of advertising appeals, however, we believe the services of an advertising agency to be indispensable. Advertising copy, design, marketing and placement call for highly expert, professional skills, and the non-specialist is unlikely to succeed in a field where competition is fierce and, given the high stakes, cost-effectiveness is difficult to achieve.

It is wise to approach a number of agencies before a final choice is made. The short-list will commend itself by the known record of the agents and the type of clients for whom they normally work. Given that the account is considered to be economically viable by the competing agencies, each of them will be only too glad to arrange a meeting to make a 'presentation' suggesting how it would run a campaign on the organisation's behalf. This provides very reasonable evidence on which to make a rational choice, and to judge whether the agency has a basic understanding of the style required. When the right agency has been chosen, it is absolutely essential that it is given a clear and comprehensive briefing, not only of the aims, objects and functions of the organisation, but also its sensibilities and the way in which it wishes to be represented.

Thereafter, the agency's copy will need careful monitoring to ensure that it continues truly to reflect the aims and ethos of the organisation, and, while possibly treading new paths to stimulate the public's interest, remains true to the basic image which the public has learnt to know and to trust. If the advertising is to be sustained over a period of years, a change of agency may well be needed if the impetus of the appeal is to be maintained.

Advertising may, of course, serve several aims simultaneously: it may seek practical rather than financial help; it may aim to publicise the aims and needs of the organisation as a spur to general fund-raising; or it may appeal directly for money. Whatever the purpose, effective advertising is extremely expensive and is therefore, perhaps, only suitable for the larger organisations. To have any hope of raising substantial funds, advertising must, in our view, be undertaken on a large scale and in order to keep the name of the organisation in the forefront of the public consciousness it must be sustained over a lengthy period. The advertisements must have impact: they must convey their message simply but effectively in such a way that the appeal is irresistible.

One of the problems in assessing the cost-effectiveness of advertising campaigns is the difficulty of relating income to specific advertisements. Charities are responsible to their members and supporters who need to be convinced that advertising expenses are justified. The agency will monitor response by 'keying' the advertisements (e.g. 'Donations to Department XYZ'), but the returns may not always show a profit, they may indeed indicate a loss. However, these figures show only immediate direct results; they cannot reflect enhanced income which may arise as a result of the greater public awareness of the needs of the organisation that has been created by the advertising campaign. It will always be a matter of judgement as to whether any overall increase in income is attributable to the advertising campaign or to a number of different factors.

Appeals to companies

Companies vary enormously in their degree of charitable giving. Some regard it as wrong to support unrelated charities out of shareholders' money, others do not. Many of the larger firms, and some of the small ones, allocate budgets to charitable giving and appoint committees to decide how the money should be spent, others contribute only as the fancy takes them. Some respond on a personal basis, others when they can see a spin-off benefit to the company. Some have links with one charity and are therefore closed to newcomers, others believe that they should share their philanthropy over the widest possible front.

Despite this variation in attitudes, charitable giving by companies, taken collectively, is very significant indeed. In response to the Royal Silver Jubilee Appeal for instance, it is estimated that at least 60 per cent of the total income of over £16 million came from companies. £8.25 million came from 750 gifts from major companies and trusts alone. This is all the more remarkable when it is remembered that such gifts are entirely discretionary. Unlike charitable trusts, companies have no obligation to give to charity at all, and the fact that they do so is very much to their credit. But it does mean that in seeking help, charities and voluntary organisations must be able to persuade the potential donors not only that they should give to their particular cause but that they should give at all. There must be a reason for the company to give. It is for the applicant to identify and bring out that reason, and to gear his approach to it.

There are, in practice, a wide variety of reasons why companies give to charities. They range from genuine altruism to blatant self-interest.

Firstly, there is the possibility that a director, owner or executive of the business (or even a relative) has a direct personal concern for a particular charity and can therefore influence company policy to the benefit of that charity. It follows that access to such people is the most effective way of winning support. No opportunity should ever be lost to involve company heads in the activities of a charitable organisation. Send information about the charity (e.g. a newsletter) regularly, invite the key people in the company to special events and functions, particularly if there is an opportunity for them to take a significant role, and always recognise, fully and properly, and if possible publicise, any gift which is received. It is a good idea to arrange a ceremony or function from time to time simply to show appreciation of the organisation's supporters.

Companies often like to feel that their money is going to a specific and identifiable purpose, where tangible results can be secured in a relatively short time. Better still if the project (e.g. an ambulance) can carry the company's name as donor.

Along the same lines, sponsorship has attractions for many firms. They prefer to be associated with a particular event rather than be one of many donors to the wider aims of a charity, and they can enjoy a measure of publicity in the process (see Chapter 10).

Companies tend to have special sympathy for local causes. Charities have the opportunity to develop friendly links in a whole variety of ways and can often appeal on a personal basis. The company knows that it is making a positive contribution to the welfare of the local community and can be seen to be doing so, and will thereby encourage local goodwill. Again it is very important that gifts should receive maximum publicity. The receipt of a cheque is an opportunity for a ceremony and for the interest of local reporters.

A lot of company giving is influenced by a desire to encourage organisations who work in fields generally helping to improve the quality of manpower, e.g. education, training, voluntary service overseas.

Some companies may be appealed to on the grounds that their business interests have something in common with the aims of the charity. Thus manufacturers of baby foods may feel a special concern for organisations seeking to promote the welfare of young children.

Joint promotions of goods may bring mutual benefits. The charity enjoys a share of the profits, the company can expect that using the charity's name on products and in advertising will encourage sales.

Wherever possible, a personal approach through well known contacts is always best. The president, chairman, secretary, trustees etc. of national organisations will have some friends in the business world and such links are invaluable. At the local level it is also likely that friendly contacts will have been established over a period of time and in a whole variety of ways.

Apart from these personal channels of communication, it will be obvious that different kinds of appeal will be required to suit a wide variety of circumstances as well as the level of donation being sought. When really large amounts are involved, our recommendation would be to proceed along the lines outlined in the section on charitable trusts (see Chapter 16). Most appeals must be made by letter. There are really two extremes of approach: a mass mailing which looks for a small percentage of respondents and in which the choice of potential donor companies is made on fairly broad guidelines; or individually written personal letters to carefully selected companies, giving specific reasons why they should respond and the benefits that they may enjoy as a consequence.

Whichever course is followed, it will be helpful to refer to directories which list and give information about companies. Locally, libraries hold copies of the year books published by the chambers of commerce, listing local member companies alphabetically and subdivided by trades, professions, etc. These are also available to non-members direct from local chambers of commerce on payment of a nominal charge to cover postage costs. Nationally, there are many suitable directories, listing companies by name, product, turnover, or location. They tend to be very expensive and quickly become obsolete. It is obviously essential to use a directory which is as up to date and therefore as accurate as possible and the sensible course is to use the services of a reference library which carries a suitably wide range. The following directories are useful to the fund-raiser.

City Directory (Cambridge: Woodhead-Faulkner (Publishers) Ltd, bi-annual).

Directory of Directors (Haywards Heath: Thomas Skinner Directories, annual).

Extel Handbook of Market Leaders (London: Extel Statistical Services Ltd, twice a year).

Financial Times International Business and Companies Year Book (London: Financial Times Ltd, annual).

Jane's Major Companies of Europe (London: Jane's Yearbooks, annual).

Kelly's Manufacturers and Merchants Directory, vol. 1, 'Great Britain—Northern Ireland' (Kingston-upon-Thames: Kelly's Directories Ltd, annual).

Kemps Directory (London: Kemps Group, annual).

Key British Enterprises (London: Dun & Bradstreet Ltd, annual). 2 vol.

Kompass United Kingdom (Haywards Heath: Kompass Publishers, annual). 2 vol.

Stock Exchange Official Year-Book (Haywards Heath: Thomas Skinner & Co. (Publishers) Ltd, annual).

Stubbs Buyers' Guide (London: Dun & Bradstreet Ltd, annual).

The Times 1000: Leading Companies in Britain and Overseas (London: Times Books, annual).

Who Owns Whom: United Kingdom and Republic of Ireland (London: Who Owns Whom Ltd, annual). 2 vol.

Also important is the use of good quality notepaper with an eye-catching heading. This establishes the basic facts about an organisation, its registered charitable status, and its distinguished supporters. It lends credibility to the organisation and therefore establishes the bona-fides of the appeal. It can also say a lot about the style of the organisation: old-fashioned or forward-looking, dyed-in-the-wool or imaginative.

On the whole, letters should be as brief as possible, consistent with presenting the essential facts and arguments. Company executives simply do not have time to wade through a lengthy presentation, however well prepared and persuasive. The typical businessman wants to be satisfied that the appeal is 'genuine' and that any money donated will be well used. He will also want to know whether there is any kudos in it for the company. He is certain to receive other appeals in the course of a year – some well-known firms get as many as 30 a day! It is a competitive situation and the appeal which is to command attention and commend itself against the others must somehow be distinctive.

Letters need to be as personal as possible, preferably addressed to a specific named individual. There are a number of impressive cases on record where individual fund-raisers, writing with conviction and forethought, have raised very large sums in this way. Conversely, standard circular letters and annual reports written to a stereotyped pattern drop into the company mail box with monotonous regularity and are easily ignored. With a large mailing this is difficult to avoid, but at least ensure that the letter is personally 'topped and tailed' by an important person in the organisation. An even better way of 'personalising' standard letters is to use a 'word-processor'. These machines are a comparatively recent development. Using continuous stationery, they allow for the automatic typing of standard letters (or standard paragraphs) and the insertion of variables, such as the name and address, *in the same type*. The more sophisticated (and expensive) machines can insert the variables automatically from prerecorded information. This is obviously desirable where many thousands of letters are to be produced. For shorter runs, the so-called 'interactive approach' is generally used, the machine stopping at the appropriate places to allow an operator to type in the variables. Machines are available to buy or to rent but are very expensive and would probably appeal only to organisations who send out a large number of letters of this kind on a regular basis. There are some bureaux who will handle this type of work but, as yet, they are few and far between.

There is some evidence that whatever means are used to give a personal touch to mass appeals to companies, they are becoming less and less effective: the strategy is suffering from overkill. It is quite obvious that only a small proportion of petitions will evoke a favourable response no matter how worthy the cause and well made the plea. This is to be expected and no one should be frustrated by failure. The fact that a company does not respond to an appeal on one occasion does not necessarily mean that the door is closed for ever. Indeed, it is hardly to be expected that they should respond to an unexpected appeal. But persistence engenders familiarity and can often bring results. Unless there are compelling reasons to the contrary, our message is to try, try and try again. It is essential therefore, to keep records of the companies approached and the results obtained as a guide to future policy, to plan the timing of a further approach, to guard against 'killing the goose' by approaching a generous donor too frequently, or to provide a mailing list for relevant information and publicity.

Charity brochures

It is worth remembering that not all company giving consists of straight donations of money. Many firms are willing to place advertisements in charity brochures and programmes which can thereby be produced to a high standard and made very attractive and saleable. The choice of a printer is very important. It is wise to obtain several estimates, since charges in the printing trade vary enormously. But cost is not the only factor. The quality of the brochure is vital; one needs a printer whose techniques are suitable to the purpose, but who is also not too big nor too professionally minded to be bothered dealing with a relatively inexpert client. The cooperation of a competent and sympathetic printer can be invaluable. He will advise on the most suitable weights and quality of paper, and of the alternative costs of producing the brochure to various specifications. When production details have been settled, the price of advertisements can be fixed, allowing for a generous profit.

As in all fund-raising, the style of approach to potential advertisers is crucial. In the first place, as ever, personal conversation with established business contacts is most likely to succeed. All members of the organisation will have some links of this kind, but they may need to be asked and will certainly need to be primed to make the approach.

Written selling of advertising space is much harder. One should plan for a very low rate of response, perhaps one in 50, and therefore send large numbers of letters to sell only a few pages. If the response is above expectations so much the better; what you cannot afford is to be undersold. The letter should set out, warmly and graphically, the details of the occasion, the aims of the organisation, the reason for the fund-raising event and what it is hoped to achieve. It should describe the brochure, and clearly demonstrate the options, special offers and printing specifications open to advertisers with their relative costs. Don't forget to indicate a realistic closing date for the receipt of copy and artwork or blocks, say a month in advance of the printer's deadline. Inevitably, there will be delay for one reason or another. From experience we know that it is vital to build in a period of grace to allow for this and to give adequate time for assembling all necessary material with every detail correct. (We recall an occasion when lack of a space and a capital letter brought ridicule. The printer had interpreted 'Te Deum in D' as 'Tedeum in D'.) Try to make the advertiser's response administratively simple by enclosing or appending an order form with the minimum amount of information requiring completion. And finish the letter with the signature of an important person which will carry far more weight than that of an unknown organiser.

A charity brochure can be an impressive piece of publicity. It affords a marvellous opportunity to set out the aims, objects and needs of the organisation with, perhaps, a personal message from a famous patron or president. Advertising in such a high-quality medium can be a matter of considerable prestige and the price of an advertisement can be varied according to where it is placed. The opportunity for really top-quality pages – say in gold or silver, perhaps matching the cover – is likely to attract companies who can afford to pay the significantly higher cost and who like to be seen as generous supporters of the charity.

The person who takes on the overall responsibility for the production of the brochure needs to be very persuasive but also to have a very conscientious eye for detail. He will have a hard and exacting task over a period of several weeks and may need the support of a small subcommittee. He needs to be readily available to advertisers, who may have various questions to raise. It is a key job in the organisation of special events and may very well produce more funds than the function itself. It should never be treated as a mere sideline to the general planning. Every telephone call, every letter, represents a potential sizeable contribution to the financial success of the whole event, and persistence and commitment here can reap a rich harvest. It is possible to raise several thousand pounds if the work is given sufficient time, dedication and reasonable skill.

If an organisation lacks an individual who has the time, ability and necessary contacts to make a success of this undoubted money-spinner there are a number of firms who specialise in the production of charity brochures including the selling of advertising space. Their fees, usually a percentage of the take (amounting to as much as 50 per cent) are high, but, in our experience, given a first-class function the net profit is still likely to be well worth while.

Company clubs

Another potential source of funds which should not be neglected is employees' sports and social clubs which may well donate funds independently of the company. Such clubs are non-profit-making and for them to run, say, a darts match for charity adds a sparkle and sense of purpose to their activities. The sums involved will be relatively small, but full recognition and gratitude at this level is one of the ways in which the greater needs of the charity can be made known. The handing over of a cheque can be made an occasion, with photographs for the house magazine and perhaps the involvement of a director in making the presentation. Great achievements can grow from small beginnings.

Broadcast appeals

Both the BBC and IBA provide time and facilities for appeals by charities.

BBC

Appeals are broadcast by radio 53 times a year ('The Week's Good Cause') and by television 14 times.

Applications may be made by any registered charity to The Appeals Secretary, British Broadcasting Corporation, Broadcasting House, London W1A 1AA. A form will be provided for the purpose, and an audited set of accounts must accompany the application (for this reason the charity must normally have been established for at least two years). An appeals advisory committee meets three times a year and gives its recommendations on which appeals should be allocated broadcasting time and whether this should be by television or radio (applicants may express a preference, but this cannot necessarily be met). The BBC tries to take account of special needs, such as timing the broadcast to coincide with an anniversary or special campaign.

The results of appeals are seldom huge, and are sometimes measured in hundreds rather than thousands of pounds. At one time television appeals were considerably more successful than those on radio, but the gap is now closing.

Independent Television

Appeal programmes are broadcast once a month on a Sunday evening. They are produced in turn by each of the four major companies that broadcast at the weekend – ATV, Granada, London Weekend and Yorkshire – and are networked throughout the United Kingdom, except in Scotland which normally has its own appeals produced by Scottish Television. During the financial

115

year 1976/77, the 12 appeals produced a total of £49,391, but six of these accounted for £36,523. In Scotland, there were 12 appeals producing a total of £6,037 and in Northern Ireland, where Ulster Television from time to time broadcasts its own local appeals, there were three programmes which raised £768.

Like the BBC, the decisions about which charities will be given broadcasting time are taken after consideration and recommendations made by an appeals advisory committee. Any organisation which has charitable status (e.g. registration with the Charity Commission) can apply for an appeal, but preference is normally given to bodies concerned with the relief of distress, the preservation of life and health, and the amelioration of social conditions. Applications should be sent to the Appeals Secretary, Independent Broadcasting Authority, 70 Brompton Road, London SW3 1EY.

Planning a broadcast appeal

A number of points apply equally to BBC and IBA broadcasts. Both have a rule which normally precludes further appeals or consideration of re-applications within a period of two years. Both bear the cost of appeal programmes, take responsibility for their format and production, and provide all necessary services and technical assistance. This usually extends to script writing in consultation, of course, with the charity. The budget for television appeals is limited, but may allow for some location shots.

Both take into consideration the charity's need of funds, and require to be satisfied that the money cannot reasonably be provided from income or from reserves. If an organisation shows substantial liquid capital in its consolidated accounts, it may be necessary to show that this money is in fact necessary as day-to-day working finance. For instance, in the case of a charity with several hundred regional branches with its working capital distributed throughout this network, the available resources to meet a special need may, in practice, be quite limited. Special circumstances such as this need to be explained when making the application.

The degree of success of an appeal programme depends, of course, on the nature of the cause, but also very much on the way it is put over. It is customary to choose a celebrity to make the appeal, and this choice is absolutely crucial. In our view, a famous personality is essential, but not all famous people have the personal qualities to win sympathy and support for a particular cause.

The preparation of a short appeal nevertheless occupies several weeks and it is necessary to ensure that one person within the charity is made responsible for arrangements and for liaison with the broadcasting organisation. The work takes up quite a lot of time and can scarcely be handled as an 'extra' job. It is a considerable privilege to be given an opportunity to appeal to a vast audience, and the broadcasting organisation has every right to expect full cooperation from the charity making the appeal.

Postal appeals

Where substantial donations are sought, there is really no substitute for personal contact. But if an appeal is to be extensive, the personal approach, however desirable, is quite impracticable. A postal appeal is the answer, but must be recognised for what it is – a decidedly blunt fund-raising tool. Unless those appealed to are already supporters, it can be reckoned that more than 90 people in every 100 will not reply; in some cases the proportion is as high as 98 per cent. It follows that the donations from the small percentage who respond must be sufficient to cover the expenses of the entire mailing and then show a profit if the exercise is to be worth while. Clearly, the aim must be to push up the percentage response as high as possible, while keeping the costs to a minimum consistent with that purpose.

Postage, paper, printing and any professional help employed are all expensive. Plainly, an appeal cannot be addressed to all and sundry and still show a worthwhile profit. The first task is to identify the groups most likely to respond. Established charities and professional 'direct mail' companies will have lists of those known to have given generously in the past, but the selection will always depend on the nature of the appeal and available resources. Possible 'target' groups are:

  (a) existing supporters;
  (b) those with a direct interest in or association with the object of the appeal;
  (c) commercial and industrial companies;
  (d) particular occupational groups;
  (e) members of churches or voluntary organisations;
  (f) people thought to be affluent, sympathetic or both;
  (g) people in a particular area, e.g. for localised projects.

One charity has conceived the novel idea of inviting contributions from people of the same name on their 'namesake day'

Ensure that your message carries maximum impact, makes the aim clear, convinces the reader of the need and leads him towards a response. Thoughtful, caring people will welcome advice on different ways of giving and how their donation can be enhanced through tax reliefs (see Chapter 7). If they are unable to afford to send cash there and then, they may nevertheless take the opportunity of giving later, or of making a bequest.

The basic rules of business letter writing apply. Before putting pen to paper, one needs to consider the restraints under which the reader works and the attitudes which colour his thinking. He is probably a very busy man, awash with paperwork, and possibly suspicious of charities and/or of 'begging letters'. Your letter must command his attention and get its message across effectively. It must convince him of the sincerity and genuineness of the organisation and the merit of the appeal's objective. If the letter is long-winded he is likely to give up before the end. Detail and technical information, though desirable, are better placed *after* the basic message, which should be direct and simple. A sensible order might be:

1. Title of the project.
2. The basic appeal (signed, if possible, by a person in the public eye and supported by the major VIPs behind the appeal).
3. The name and address of the organisation and a statement of its credentials and aims.
4. How much is needed, and suggestions of ways help can be given.
5. Simple advice on the benefits accruing from covenanted donations.
6. Provision to complete a deed of covenant and banker's order or a simple donation slip (these might be better as separate enclosures).

Use photographs or illustrations if they help to make the message clear or increase its effectiveness. Follow the ordinary rules of good style: use plain words and keep the reader firmly in mind. Avoid jargon, complicated phrases, and overlong sentences and paragraphs. Always finish by pointing the reader towards the response you seek.

It is unlikely that one standard letter will be appropriate for everybody. Try to relate the style of appeal to the varying groups of potential donors. It may be worth while to employ professional help for both copy and layout. But the costs must be carefully weighed against the likely return. The use of a 'word processor', as mentioned previously (page 112), can considerably improve the appearance of the letter and give it a personal touch.

Try to arrange for your appeal to arrive at a convenient time and, if possible, when the living is easy: for salaried workers this usually means at the beginning of each month or after a beneficent Budget. Many charities choose the season of goodwill to all men, despite the competition, but make sure you don't leave it until all the spare cash has gone on presents!

It is important to say thank you, despite the additional cost. You may have won a regular donor.

14. Campaigns and consultants

We juxtapose these two aspects of fund-raising deliberately. While it would be quite wrong to say that you can't have one without the other, they nevertheless share common ground in that both are most commonly used on short-term projects – situations in which a lot of money is needed in a short time.

Using consultants

Consultants deal in expertise. They advise on how to organise and mount a campaign and where to cast the fund-raising nets. While they will direct and sustain a campaign, they will not normally seek funds directly. They rely on the organisation to provide its own labour force and to do the donkey-work of fund-raising. They thrive, essentially, because many organisations needing money quickly do not have the time, the knowledge or the resources to set up and carry through a successful major campaign on their own initiative.

At their best, fund-raising consultants have a considerable reputation and can be said to have revolutionised fund-raising in the post-war years (if somewhat against the grain of traditional British thinking). They offer a range of skills and a knowledge of fund-raising techniques which are otherwise hard to find, extending to press and public relations, advertising and the production of promotional literature and appeals. Hardly less important are their contacts with professional associates in such fields as market research, the graphic arts, photography and film production.

As in all spheres of business activity, however, there are good and bad practitioners and the usual grey area. Anyone can set up as a fund-raising consultant, and no guarantee of success can be given. Fees are usually payable whether or not the objects of the campaign are achieved and are often unrelated to the sums raised.

Bearing in mind that consultants' services are expensive, we suggest that if expert professional help is indispensable, consideration should first be given to whether it might not be more cost-effective to take on a suitable full-time employee for the purpose. The right person can provide a stimulus to fund-raising not merely for a special campaign but over the whole range of regular fund-raising activities on a long-term basis and, it is to be hoped, with a deeper sense of involvement with the purposes of the organisation than one can reasonably expect from an outside consultant with many other clients. If this course of action is not possible or appropriate, then at least choose a consultant with care: be satisfied that the firm has good 'form'. You would not, after all, take on any key member of staff without references and proof of professional competence: no more should you take a fund-raising consultant on trust or on the strength of a smart brochure.

With or without professional help, a short-term fund-raising campaign must be what is called 'intensive'. If some of our readers shrink from this word, it is a feeling which we come close to sharing. For intensive methods carry dangers. They can imply aggressive, hard-selling techniques – the sort of persuasions normally associated with encyclopedia salesmen. We recently heard of a professional fund-raiser who spoke openly of 'milking' his target donors! Such methods may well succeed. They may bring in big money. But for every donation won, there may be several potential supporters antagonised, and the prospects of enjoying continued and sustained financial help may be seriously damaged. Thus the long-term effects on a responsible charity may well offset any immediate advantage.

Planning a campaign

Having sounded this note of caution, however, it must be recognised that a campaign to raise substantial and abnormal amounts of money must of necessity be intensive. It is no use thinking of a target sum, making an appeal, and then sitting back hoping that the money will turn up from somewhere. A campaign is, by definition, an *organised* course of *action*. It requires:

(*a*) a realistic assessment of needs (including the expenses of the campaign and allowing for inflation);

(*b*) a target to meet those needs;

(*c*) the setting up of a high-powered campaign team and, if the appeal is to encompass a large area, regional organisers;

(*d*) identification and appraisal of alternative potential sources of funds;

(*e*) an all-out, sustained and positive drive to reach the goal.

The available fund-raising techniques are numerous and diverse and have been described in earlier chapters. Some will commend themselves more readily than others in the context of seeking quick and substantial returns. There are no hard and fast rules. A charity with many branches throughout the country may rely primarily on the local efforts of many thousands of members: a veritable fund-raising army. If 300 branches can be inspired to raise only £2000 each, the return is prodigious. Other organisations, not able to muster this kind of support, may look to wealthy philanthropists and grant-making trusts, press campaigns and postal appeals.

The aim must be a genuine one – clearly defined and set out. If funds are sought for, say, research into the cause and cure of a disease, it is not sufficient to say that £x are required for 'medical research'. There must be a clear and positive prospectus of exactly how the money will be spent. Potential private donors will want to know how their money is to be used, and grant-making bodies will not be impressed by vague good intentions.

Many charities find it worth while to call a press conference to launch the campaign. There is advice on this form of publicity in Chapter 12.

It helps, of course, if the aim is one which commands wide support and sympathy. It is likely to be easier to raise funds to provide holidays for deprived children than to restore a church roof. But any aim is bound to have its natural allies and a major part of the success of any campaign lies in winning their patronage and involvement.

If famous people will lend their names to the appeal it will gain status accordingly. People are naturally suspicious of any demand upon their purse, and the support of respected members of society helps to inspire confidence and establish the genuineness of the campaign. Nothing succeeds like success and each donor won is an exemplar to encourage the others.

Good campaign literature is very important – it needs to be eye-catching, informative and persuasive. It should convey not only what the aim is, but how that aim will be achieved. It should not merely appeal for money, but show how a donation will be used in practice. It should point out what has been achieved already (and hence needs to be updated throughout the campaign) and imply unshakeable confidence in the way ahead. It should bring home the fact – honestly and without triviality – that the need is both irresistible and imperative. It should unlock jaded sympathies and untie purse strings.

This kind of enthusiasm, of course, comes naturally when the organisers believe in what they are seeking to achieve and are genuinely committed to their task. Fund-raisers who share the ethos of the organisation they represent are also far more likely to convince and involve those whose help they seek. We believe that a fund-raising campaign has been successful not merely when the financial target has been reached, but when fund-raisers and donors alike can look back with satisfaction at what they have helped to achieve and forward with pride to the fruits of their endeavour.

Case history of a fund-raising campaign

We feel it may be helpful to give an example of an actual campaign, and we are indebted to the Winged Fellowship Trust for permission to give a broad outline of their highly successful Essex appeal. We do not claim that this is a standard recipe for success – results depend not only on the methods used, but on the prowess, commitment and flair of the fund-raisers, the support which they enjoy within the community, and the degree of sympathy with which the appeal is generally received. No two campaigns are exactly alike, and the Essex appeal is put forward not as a model, but to show how a campaign strategy was tailored to fit particular circumstances and to illustrate some of the factors which might be regarded as useful ingredients in other appeals.

The aim was clear: to provide a first-class holiday home for severely disabled people at Grange Farm, Chigwell, Essex. In seeking to fulfil this objective, the Trust, under the patronage of HRH Princess Alice, Duchess of Gloucester, and with an impressive roll of trustees, could boast impeccable credentials. It already operated a holiday centre for disabled people at Crabhill House, Surrey, which had been the subject of a BBC television documentary. National recognition of the work of the Trust had been marked by the first of three annual grants of £4000 from the Department of Health and Social Security.

A holiday centre already existed at Grange Farm and a summer season had operated there for 15 years, but the accommodation was limited and rather rudimentary. It had been a long-term ambition to build a more permanent and better equipped home. A strong support committee existed which had a widespread network of voluntary helpers to call on, many of whom had been supporting the Trust for all of that time. Also, a local fund-raising committee had been formed for some time and between these two committees money had been raised regularly from local sources. Through central and local efforts, a substantial sum, nearly £100,000, had been raised in advance of the main appeal.

Thus the Trust had established its credentials, proven its ability to carry out its objectives, and built a firm foundation, not only of money, but of support and goodwill. The significance of these factors to any campaign can hardly be overstated.

In 1974, a new site at Grange Farm was offered by the City Parochial Foundation and was gratefully accepted. At a time of rapid inflation and escalating building costs, it was realised that if the projected holiday home was to become a reality the necessary additional capital would need to be raised quickly. So planning permission was obtained and in 1975 the Essex appeal was launched under the patronage of the Lord Lieutenant of the county. By December 1977, the home – a particularly attractive modern building in open country – was open to disabled guests: a truly remarkable achievement. How was it done?

In the first place, given a very small permanent staff and limited resources, the Trust decided against the use of professional consultants and committed themselves to 'go it alone'. The campaign was developed on two fronts: a central drive directed by the well-connected trustees, whose efforts brought in a number of bedrock gifts from private, industrial and commercial donors, and a wider strategy under the control of a campaign organiser and two part-time assistants all dedicated to their task. A wide-ranging postal appeal was rejected on grounds of expense, but intelligent and effective use was made of the *Directory of Grant-Making Trusts* (see page 137) in selecting trusts relevant to the cause and able to help.

Approaches to other voluntary organisations on the basis of suggesting a visit to explain personally what the Trust was seeking to achieve were invariably successful and secured both wide support and significant contributions. Groups like Rotary Clubs and Round Tables were ready to lend their support in raising funds: they were able to feel a sense of sharing a common purpose in so obvious a service to the community. They also liked, it has to be said, the 'non-professional' approach and the conspicuous absence of slick public relations techniques. These exploratory meetings were nevertheless expertly conducted and greatly assisted by the use of a scale model of the holiday home.

Because of its very limited permanent staff, the Winged Fellowship Trust had to be extraordinarily efficient in the organisation of the appeal. In concentrating their efforts within the county of Essex, they were able not only to operate within a reasonably confined area but could appeal to the natural sympathies of local residents towards a project proceeding in their own county. Ordinary people could help in a whole variety of ways, and imaginative leaflets set out the choices and invited support. Apart from a straightforward donation, they could, for example, become 'Friends of Grange Farm' for as little as £5 a year, take a collecting box, organise a regular collection, or, for young people, fill up an attractive 'brick card' by selling stick-on stamps at 5p each.

A very important feature of the wider fund-raising strategy was the establishment of a network of voluntary chairmen throughout the county, organising local fund-raising. These were hand-picked individuals, covering a wide range of interests, respected in their own spheres and with the right kind of stature and influence to win support in their own communities. Acting largely on their own initiative, but with the constant support and encouragement of the campaign organiser and a small secretarial staff, they made an extremely effective fund-raising team, stimulating and harnessing the enthusiasm of local groups in a wide variety of activities. There were many unusual ideas, such as sponsored sunflower growing by children in primary schools. With the blessing of the local education authority, a few seeds per child, with instructions for their cultivation, flowered to the extent of £10,000.

But a much deeper selective analysis was essential for larger contributions, and the mainspring of this was to consider how the holiday home could help other groups, who would thus find a donation beneficial to themselves as well as to the Trust. Valuable support was attracted by offering both voluntary and statutory organisations caring for disabled people long-term booking privileges in return for a once-only capital donation. For local groups lacking the resources to build and staff a holiday home themselves, the Winged Fellowship's proposals were positively welcome.

The campaign literature was bright, attractive and well designed. It spelled out the objective clearly and simply and left no doubt about how help could be given. Particularly telling was the linking of various levels of contribution with specific results. Thus £5 would meet the cost of one day of a disabled guest's holiday, £15 a weekend, £35 a week and so on. Larger contributions were promoted as conferring special benefits such as the right to choose a name for a room, or, as we have mentioned, to reserve a place for the exclusive use of severely disabled people in one's own area or organisation.

But the outstanding feature of the whole campaign, in our judgement, was the decision to commence building before all the necessary capital had been raised. There is no doubt in our minds that the campaign gathered momentum and strength because donors knew where their money was going – into a live project and not a dead bank. It was a bold move, not without risk, but Jubilee Lodge at Grange Farm, occupied and serving the needs of people with severe disabilities, now proudly justifies the faith of those who made it possible.

15. Other fund-raising ideas

The Alexandra Day Fund

The Alexandra Day Fund was founded in 1912 to benefit the sick, the aged, children, and disabled and infirm people. It raises money in two main ways. First and foremost by street collections held all over the UK, as well as in Canada and New Zealand, when the famous rose emblems, first suggested by Her late Majesty Queen Alexandra, are given in recognition of donations; and secondly, throughout the year, by means of sponsored events organised by a Special Events Campaign Team.

The Fund is a major national organisation (now under the presidency of HRH Princess Alexandra) which raises money specifically to support independent charities dedicated to the relief of human distress. Alexandra Day collects around £200,000 every year and is thus an important source of funds for appropriate charities. It lends support to over 700 charities in the Greater London area alone and many thousands more in other parts of the country.

The Special Events Campaign team organises and mounts a programme of sponsored events throughout the country, and individuals are encouraged to take part to raise money for a charity of their choice. Organisations are given the opportunity to invite people to take part in a sponsored event to raise funds on their behalf. The sponsored individual indicates, on the sponsor form provided by the Alexandra Day Fund, the charity he has nominated and between 50 and 60 per cent of the money he raises will be forwarded to that charity. (The remainder goes to the charities regularly supported by the Fund.) The fund usually distributes posters around the town to announce the event and will supply leaflets and posters to any interested organisation. With all administrative responsibilities being borne by the Alexandra Day Fund it is obviously an excellent idea to encourage young people to run, jog, swim, etc. for the financial benefit of your organisation.

The Special Events team is always ready to talk to groups to explain the details of any event.

Appeals for help from the Alexandra Day Fund or for the organisation of sponsored events should be made to Alexandra Rose Day, 1 Castelnau, Barnes, London SW13 9RP.

Carnival novelties

It has not been our policy to recommend the products of any particular firm as aids to fund-raising. We feel, however, that exception must be made in favour of Barnum's Carnival Novelties Ltd of 67 Hammersmith Road, London W14 8UY (telephone 01 602 1211), for their catalogue of (what else?) carnival novelties and fund-raising paraphernalia is a treasure-house without parallel. Here are balloons, printed pens and pencils, key fobs and pottery mugs, hats, funny noses, masks, games and fête equipment galore. There is a special section devoted entirely to equipment for fund-raising, fêtes and fairs. A list of over 100 categories includes advertising and street banners, collecting boxes, raffle drums and tickets, tombola sheets, bingo books, flags, specially printed badges, banners, signs and flag day emblems, coconut shies and wooden balls, hoop-la rings, and a host of other familiar games.

Celebrities

Personalities from the worlds of show business and sport can add lustre to a wide variety of fund-raising occasions and can, of course, make a really significant difference to the attendance figures. It is important to appreciate, however, that not all entertainers are prepared to give their services free: some, it is cynically suggested, make their entire living from charity performances.

If you wish to invite a celebrity to a fund-raising function or to take part in a concert in aid of charity, there are a few basic factors which should be borne in mind.

1. Really top performers work to very tight schedules. Invitations need to be extended well in advance.
2. Don't invite 'stars' to minor events. Not only is this an abuse of their kindness and a waste of their time, but it represents a failure to use their 'pulling power' to the full.
3. Give the celebrity some consideration. You cannot reasonably expect him to travel half the length of the country to suit your arrangements. Rather plan your event to suit his programme, if possible when he is appearing locally, when it

should be relatively easy for him to fit in a charity appearance. Alternatively, if the date is fixed, telephone the local theatre or sports organisers, to find out who is appearing there on that day, and make your request accordingly.

4. Treat your famous guest with courtesy and respect – keep him informed of what you are trying to achieve and give him the opportunity to play a real part in achieving it. Celebrities are people and, if ready to help at all, will want to help positively and to be involved.

The chain-reaction principle

This principle can be applied to a variety of fund-raising activities. In its simplest form, if one person not only contributes 10p to a charitable project but persuades two other people to do the same – i.e. to contribute 10p each and each to persuade two other people to do the same – the effect is that the contribution at each stage doubles (Figure 15.1).

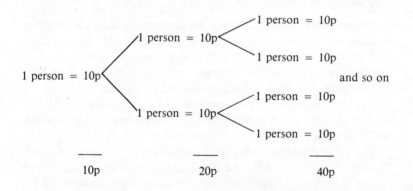

The effect is a geometric progression. After only ten stages, the total collected is £102.30. Of course there are snags, but even if the chain fails here and there, the total collection can be considerable.

The same principle can be applied to, say, a coffee morning. Eight guests contribute 50p each, then organise their own coffee morning inviting another eight people, and so on.

First stage:	1 coffee morning	£4.00
Second stage:	8 coffee mornings	£32.00
Third stage:	64 coffee mornings	£256.00
Fourth stage:	512 coffee mornings	£2048.00

Eventually, in theory, the whole population will be at a coffee morning!

Cheese and wine parties

The English Country Cheese Council, National Dairy Centre, John Princes Street, London W1M 0AP will supply on request a range of leaflets giving advice on arranging fund-raising cheese and wine parties, together with catering hints, ideas and recipes for making the party a success. They will also supply some colourful display material and English cheese tags to identify the cheeses on your party table. Give the date of the party, the approximate numbers attending, and allow two weeks for delivery.

W. E. Tucker Ltd, Twinstead, Sudbury, Suffolk supply information and guidance via the National Milk Publicity Council Inc. on organising fund-raising parties: the printing and sale of tickets in advance, the purchase, choice and serving of drinks, ideas for food from the traditional cheese and wine to buffet meals, and some tips on running a raffle.

Community festivals

In recent years, there has been an upsurge in the popularity of community festivals, culminating in the nationwide street parties and celebrations which marked Her Majesty the Queen's silver jubilee. Pageants and processions, carnivals and field days have been with us for years, but have been mainly spectator sports. The present-day trend is towards recreating the continental *feu de joie* of earlier times and involving people, young and old, in a joyful and colourful occasion.

The primary purpose of such festivities may not be to raise money, but they nevertheless provide a wonderful opportunity to do so in a whole variety of ways, without at all dampening the revelry. Stalls and side-shows can provide entertainment *and* show a profit. Our experience is that people are attracted to stalls which offer fun and amusement with the chance of a prize, rather that just a straightforward gamble – none more so, alas, than throwing wet sponges at the heads of fellow human beings or aiming at a target which, if a bullseye is scored, tips a bucket of water over an unfortunate person strategically placed below. Having said this, of course, bingo and tombola remain firm favourites with many people.

Raffles are also well supported if the prizes are attractive, the cause is favoured, and the sale of tickets is well organised and publicised. Souvenir programmes are a very good idea and preferable to charging admission which involves problems of control and takes away from the spirit of freedom. Moreover, they can be sold beforehand to people who don't actually come to the festival. Not too lavish, perhaps, but given the support of local advertisers and a generous local printer a worthwhile brochure can be produced to sell at a price which will ensure a good return on cost.

The sale of refreshments is another obviously indispensable requirement to keep up the spirits of the merrymakers, while also providing a good margin of profit if efficiently organised.

At the end of the day, you will not have made a fortune – but that is not the object of the exercise.

An extremely useful guide for anyone planning a community festival or for that matter a more traditional fête, barbecue or even a social, is the *Community Festivals Handbook*, price 50p, available from Young Volunteer Force, 60 Highbury Grove, London N5; telephone 01 226 5375. As well as giving guidance on planning and organising a festival, it has some very sound advice on sources of finance (with specimen costings), publicity, and a variety of practical and legal problems which may be encountered. A very good half pound's worth.

Community service units

One of the problems of organising fund-raising events is that there are seldom sufficient hands to do the work. In the community service organisation there exists a task force ready and willing to help, whose very purpose is to serve on genuine projects for the benefit of the community, and whose organisers are looking for local groups and organisations within which they can work.

The community service scheme was introduced following a report in June 1970 by the Home Secretary's Advisory Council on the Penal System. The concept is to order offenders to carry out service to the community as an alternative to a prison sentence. Under the scheme, courts may require an adult who has been convicted of an offence punishable by imprisonment to carry out a community task for a total of not less than 40 nor more than 240 hours within a 12-month period. Such an order can only be made following consideration of a social enquiry report about the individual's suitability for the scheme, his willingness to conform to its demands and the availability of tasks suited to his abilities.

A great deal of effort has been made to gain the cooperation of voluntary and other bodies who might offer work opportunities for offenders on community service. The facilities available will, of course, vary according to local circumstances. Our own local CSU is able to undertake printing, including the silk-screen printing of posters, and carpentry work, for example, making stalls for fêtes. Strong hands will usually be available to assist with setting up stalls and side-shows, helping with gymkhanas and other arduous fund-raising events.

The local CSU organiser is always a member of the Probation Service and can be contacted through the local probation office. He in turn is eager to expand his local contacts with Rotary Clubs and other charitable organisations involved in service to the community.

Drum majorettes

These attractive and talented young ladies will lend colour, glamour and excitement to a wide variety of indoor and outdoor fund-raising events. The strength of the movement in Britain is steadily growing and troupes are always ready and willing to perform at suitable events organised by charities and voluntary organisations. Further information from the General Secretary, Mrs J.A. Terry, British Majorette Association, 48 Brancaster Road, Newbury Park, Ilford, Essex.

Fashion shows

Always popular, especially with the ladies, fashion shows are quite easy to arrange. You need, of course, suitable premises and the co-operation of a leading dress shop or department store, but these should not be difficult to secure. Such events are sure-fire winners for retailers, giving them a marvellous opportunity for advertising to a captive audience.

The fund-raising potential is limited, but it is one more opportunity to bring your name and your cause before the public. It is from such publicity – from the evidence of a lively and imaginative organisation – that supporters are attracted and funds begin to flow. So let the show be the best possible show that you and the shop can provide: congenial surroundings, a good compère (very important), and attractive models, preferably of both sexes and of a wide age range including some children. The success of a fashion show is largely a matter of imaginative presentation and flair, but the crowning touch might well be provided if you can interest an up-and-coming hairdresser to create hairstyles for the models. Needless to say, don't miss out on the pre-show publicity and have the tickets ready in good time to ensure the maximum attendance. Expenses should be quite modest, but it is wise to see to it that the clothes are insured.

'Friends' and helpers

'Friends' or supporter members provide invaluable support to charities and voluntary organisations, and it is a very good idea to formalise these links in a tangible way. Many people will respond to a personal invitation to become a friend on payment of an annual subscription – but they need to be asked, and most people like to be told how much they are expected to contribute as a minimum. There may be scope for 'junior friends' at a modest subscription and, for new organisations, 'founder friends' in recognition of a once-only donation set at a suitably high level (better still, persuade them to covenant their subscription by banker's order). Enrolment as a friend should confer certain benefits, perhaps a badge or car sticker to identify the subscriber with the organisation, free copies of any newsletter or magazine, and invitations to special meetings and functions. Certainly, every opportunity should be taken to involve friends in the activities of the organisation and to keep them informed of all important developments.

Other people, though unwilling or unable to help financially, may be ready to lend their services in a whole variety of ways, and this can, of course, be even more valuable than straight subscriptions. They too should be encouraged to feel that they *belong* to the organisation and are kept abreast of all its activities, so that they feel part of a team striving to achieve its primary objectives.

It is absolutely essential in respect of both friends and helpers to maintain a card index of names, addresses and telephone numbers. This will provide a basis for sending out information and any special appeals. If suitably annotated, it will ensure that supporters are not asked for help too often nor asked for help in ways which they find objectionable, for example, by being invited to buy draw tickets when they object to gambling. Thus a card may be noted:

(*a*) always ready to buy dance tickets;
(*b*) reluctant to sell raffle tickets;
(*c*) flag-day collector;
(*d*) Jubilee appeal sent ——;
(*e*) donated £*x* on ——;
(*f*) will help with catering.

The index should be kept under constant review and your aim

133

should be to build up the support it represents consistently and constantly. Friends and helpers are the first line of support for any charitable enterprise or special appeal and as such they need to be respected and nurtured.

Green Shield Community Savings Plan

The Green Shield Trading Stamp Co. Ltd, Green Shield House, Station Road, Edgware, Middlesex HA8 7AQ, offers an admirable scheme to assist voluntary groups to raise funds for genuine community projects. The group must first apply for registration with Green Shield on a form designed for the purpose, supplied on request with a booklet, *Saving for Others*. The group must establish its credentials by providing references from responsible people in their locality such as a minister of religion, headmaster, Justice of the Peace, Member of Parliament, or doctor. Green Shield will register groups who satisfy them that they want to save their trading stamps for charitable, educational or social purposes, and that their project will be of benefit to the community. Over 10,000 different organisations have already been registered in this way for projects large and small. One scheme, supported by Millicent Martin, resulted in a collection of 19 million stamps which were used to build and equip a research laboratory.

Once registered, the group can ask Green Shield for a quotation of how many books will be required to 'pay' for their project target (cash is *not* accepted). There is a target form for this purpose, and Green Shield will do its utmost to obtain whatever it is the group has set its sights on, which may or may not be a normal catalogue item. Special purchases of equipment or furniture are, however, subject to a minimum retail value of £250.

When exchanged for goods, a discount of one free book is allowed in every ten, subject to a minimum of 360 books. In some cases, Green Shield may also be able to help by obtaining the goods at an advantageous price. If the group prefers, the stamps can be exchanged for cash, but only at the normal rate of 42½p. This will not give such good value, but may be desirable where cash is being raised in a whole variety of ways for some large-scale project.

Green Shield assist the group in a number of ways to reach their target. They give helpful advice on organising the appeal in their explanatory booklet and in ideas lists and campaign suggestion lists, and will also supply a wealth of free publicity material, posters, progress charts, car stickers, collection boxes and bags, letterheadings and envelopes. There are hundreds of ways in which stamps can be collected – many people who can ill-afford to part with money will willingly give stamps. Approached properly, local shops, garages and supermarkets who give Green Shield stamps to their customers will display posters and leave a collecting box on the counter or check-out for customers who don't want the stamps for themselves.

Thousands of groups and charities have already realised their ambitions. Minibuses, guide dogs, wheelchairs and many other much-needed aids and services have been supplied in this way, and many organisations have testified how quickly and easily the stamps mount up once the scheme is set in motion.

Money makes money

This is an idea which we first came across in church fund-raising, some years ago, but which clearly has wider application and considerable potential. It is based on the parable of the talents in St Matthew's Gospel, chapter 25.

A man, about to travel to a far country, distributed various sums of money to each of his three servants according to their abilities. One servant, who had received five talents (with a present-day value of over £1000), went and traded with them and made a further five. Another, who had received two talents, similarly gained two more. But the one who received only one talent (being of least ability) dug a hole and buried it for safety. Needless to say, when the master returned he was much appreciative of the first two servants, but the third, although he had kept the money safely, was denounced as a 'wicked and slothful servant' who should at least have invested the money and gained the interest.

The application of this parable to fund-raising is bold and imaginative. Sums of money are loaned to members and supporters with the exhortation that, like the more able servants, they will return it after a stipulated period, with something added. This presents a clear challenge to work positively for the organisation. People will generally respond to such a challenge according to their abilities and invariably with at least some measure of profit. The possibilities are endless, and considerable ingenuity will undoubtedly have been demonstrated before the loans are called in.

When the Robinson family was asked to support its local church in this way, everybody helped. Young Tom was given £1 and raised another £2 by buying seeds and growing vegetables in the back garden. Fred Robinson, always a good handiman, received £10, bought a book of old prints cheaply, framed them and made a substantial profit. The mother of the family found it no great effort to bake lots of her superb fruit cakes and turned £10's worth of ingredients into £20 at the Christmas bazaar. Uncle George took himself off to the Sunday market at Brick Lane, unearthed a pair of dirty old candlesticks and some other brassware, cleaned it all up and sold the now shining antiques at 500% profit. Uncle John ("something in the City") was given £100. He bought and sold shares and, miraculously it seemed, was able to return £180 three months later. Grandma Robinson bought wool with her £10 and her knitting needles clicked to the tune of £25's worth of cardigans and jumpers. Only Grandad let the side down. He went off to the betting shop with his £10 and lost the lot. But when the reckoning came, he covered up his shame by donating £15 of his own money. No one actually buried the cash in the ground, and the vicar was able to announce that, as a result of families like the Robinsons, £5000 had become £12,000.

16. Grant-aid

Grants from charitable trusts

A very important potential source of funds, particularly for societies which find difficulty in attracting wide public sympathy and support, is the vast wealth held in trust by grant-making charities. There are over 2000 such bodies in England and Wales alone, distributing a total amount approaching £200 million. In 1972, the assets of only 50 of the major trusts or foundations were reckoned to exceed £712 million.

Charitable trusts are bound by law and by their own trust deeds to limit their philanthropy to defined objectives. There is some scope for varying these objectives in special circumstances (the principle of *cy près*) but there is an overriding criterion in law that the charitable intent must be beneficial to 'the community'. Normally, trusts are set up and operate to meet areas of special need, and are thus of exceptional interest to those who are trying to raise funds for particular charitable purposes. In seeking help, however, it is clearly essential to approach trusts whose own purposes are relevant to those of the applicant. It is no use applying for help in building a holiday home for disabled people to a trust devoted to the advancement of education.

Many trusts include among their stated objects 'general charitable purposes'. This can be misleading. The description is commonly inserted to give the trust legal elbow room rather than as an accurate statement of its actual policy.

An invaluable – indeed indispensable – guide in identifying trusts that might be prepared to help particular areas of need is the *Directory of Grant-Making Trusts* published by the Charities Aid Foundation. This covers all areas of voluntary activity and provides information under four headings:

1. Classification of charitable purposes
2. Analysis of specimen grants made.
3. Register of grant-making charitable trusts.

4. Indices (including a geographical index).

The directory is not, however, exhaustive. It excludes very small trusts and, more importantly, trusts which are based outside England and Wales. But apart from these exceptions, prospective applicants are provided with relevant details of charitable trusts, including any in their own locality, their specific objects and policy, the limits of their beneficial area and any other restrictions, their financial assets, and an indication of the scale of grants normally made. Advice is also given on how and when applications should be made. Obviously the directory can never be totally accurate and up to date, but it is regularly revised and it is sound common sense to use the most recent edition. The Charities Aid Foundation is also able to provide information from an extensive computer data bank. A print-out by subject or by geographical area can be supplied as required.

It is a good idea to make a preliminary approach to a trust in advance of a formal application, making absolutely certain that it is appropriate to what you have in mind and will be able to consider your appeal. You can explain your ideas and needs in broad outline and seek guidance on how best and when to make the application. If this is done sincerely and tactfully, possibly in person, the chances of success may well be enhanced.

It is no easy matter to secure a grant, particularly if a new venture is involved and past achievements cannot be cited. To have any hope of convincing others, the applicants must be absolutely clear in their own minds about what they intend to do and how they intend to do it. An application should not be a medium for exploring possibilities and ideas, but for definite and practicable proposals. An essential prerequisite, therefore, is a period of exacting research so that when the time is right, a convincing and coherent case can be put forward. Trustees will certainly want to be satisfied not only that the project is a worthwhile, imaginative and forward-looking concept, bringing benefit to as many people as possible, but that the applicants have the necessary expertise, competence and enthusiasm to carry it through and to make the maximum use of a grant.

Even where these criteria are satisfied, it may be necessary to progress by degrees, by first winning the support and encouragement of experienced people who are likely to be in a position to give advice on how to proceed and to help in putting the case forward. If, through personal contact, such people can be convinced and won over by the merits of the proposals and the sincerity and skill with which they are advanced, and can be persuaded to promote and advocate the project, enormous credibility and weight will be added to a formal application. Doors which can prove to be insuperable obstacles to those who approach a trust from 'cold', are thus unlocked and opened.

It follows, of course, that there is no room for the mass mailing technique when applying to trusts. Each application must be carefully tailored to suit the known characteristics of the recipients. As with any application, it pays to present the main facts concisely, not to hide them in a jungle of detailed argument. One's case is not helped if the key points can only be gleaned by reading page after page of information. It is therefore sensible to place supporting evidence (e.g. annual reports and accounts) as appendices to a relatively simple submission. This should never follow a stereotyped pattern, but we would suggest that the following information should be covered:

(*a*) the structure, staffing, function and 'history' of the organisation; why it was set up, what it has already achieved, and the continuing relevance of its aims and objects.

(*b*) how funds are raised and administered, and who is responsible for their management.

(*c*) a *realistic* appraisal of the development or project for which additional money is required, who is responsible for it, and how, given the money, it will be achieved.

(*d*) how much money is needed in what period.

(*e*) the nature and extent of the help you are seeking from the trust.

(*f*) how you are trying to raise money in other ways, and the degree to which this has been successful.

(*g*) arrangements for monitoring and publicising progress.

On the whole, we think that trustees try to be scrupulously fair, but funds are limited and are sometimes earmarked for several years in advance. Grants cannot be dispensed *ad libitum* and hard choices must be made. Many worthy applications must be rejected or restricted.

Grants from the European Social Fund

The scope of this Fund is more limited than might appear from its title. Its basic purpose (Article 123 of the EEC Treaty) is to render the employment of workers easier and to increase their geographical and occupational mobility within the Community. Eligible projects are thus explicitly related to employment – mounting and running vocational courses, assisting participation in training, changes of residence to take up new work etc. There is, however, one area of grant-aid which could well be of value to voluntary organisations that represent handicapped people. This is in favour of measures to eliminate 'obstacles which make it difficult for certain categories of disadvantaged workers to take up available employment' and specifically includes 'necessary costs of adapting jobs to handicapped persons and for the re-habilitation of handicapped persons with a view to their acquiring trade or professional skills', but *excludes* medical costs.

To qualify for Social Fund aid, schemes in the private sector need the prior support of the relevant national authority (for projects relating to handicapped people, the Department of Health and Social Security) and the final approval of the Commission of the European Communities. The EEC legislation then provides for joint financing by the Social Fund, the national authority and the private organisation. It is a condition that the national authority concerned guarantees the completion of the scheme. The contribution of the Social Fund in such cases is 'an amount equal to any expenditure taken over by the public authorities'.

Until recently, cash from the Fund was paid out only as a refund of money already spent. As from 1 January 1978, however, 30 per cent of the agreed aid, on the basis of unit costs, is paid as an advance; a further 30 per cent is paid at the halfway stage, and the remainder on completion of the project, based on proven expenditure.

For organisations planning to build and equip, say, a day centre for disabled people, this source of funds could be of inestimable value, translating a dream into a reality. Applications should, in the first instance, be made to the Department of Health and Social Security, Alexander Fleming House, Elephant and Castle, London SE1 6BY, *before carrying out any operation*, indicating that grant aid is sought from the European Social Fund. If supported, the application is forwarded to the Commission of the European Communities. The Commission decides whether assistance can be given and informs the DHSS. The following basic information is required:

(*a*) identity and status of the person responsible for financing and carrying out the operations.

(*b*) description of the operational plan, in particular its objectives, methods, duration and technical details.

(c) categories of persons concerned.

(d) estimated costs.

(e) method of financing, and yearly instalments of expenditure.

(f) types of aid proposed to be put into use.

(g) any other information which may be useful for appraising the significance and effectiveness of the operation, e.g. job opportunities created.

(h) procedures proposed for any necessary checking of the effective fulfilment of the plan.

Up to the time of writing, ten voluntary organisations have been successful in their applications to the Social Fund. These include Queen Elizabeth's Foundation for the Disabled, Inter-Action Trust, three Welsh committees for educationally subnormal young people in Mid Glamorgan, and the Scottish Craftsmanship Association.

Fuller details are given in the relevant EEC legal documents, listed below, and in the booklet *Grants and Loans from the European Community* (UK edition) published by the Commission of the European Communities. Further information is available from the European Community's Press and Information Office, 20 Kensington Palace Gardens, London W8 4QQ; telephone 01 727 8090.

The Department of Employment also publishes its own detailed booklet, *The European Social Fund: A Guide to Possible Applicants*. Copies of the booklet and advice on application can be readily obtained from Mrs Margaret Ellison, Social Fund Division, Department of Employment, 32 St James's Square, London SW1. Contact with the Department may save potential applicants wasting valuable effort in formulating claims and is strongly advised.

Law

Council Decision 71/66/EEC especially Articles 5 and 8.

Regulation 2396/71, especially Articles 3(2)(e) and 5.

Regulation 2397/71, especially Article 1, items C10 and 11.

Regulation 2398/71 (covers assistance for self-employed handicapped persons).

Financial Regulation 72/165/EEC.

Regulation 858/72 (administrative and financial procedures).

Local authority grants

Most local authority services which operate under statutory powers have specific powers to make grants to voluntary organisations; for example, the social services have such powers under the Children Act 1948, s. 46, the National Assistance Act 1948, s. 30 and 31, and the National Health Service Act 1946, s. 28.

Similar powers are provided in other Acts for other services, for example, recreation and amenities. If no specific power exists in a particular area, authorities can fall back on s. 137 of the Local Government Act 1972, which allows them to incur expenditure, not otherwise provided for, which in their opinion will be 'in the interest of their area or any part of it or all or some of its inhabitants'. The 'long-stop' provisions of the 1972 Act are subject to a limit in any one financial year equal to the product of a rate of 2p in the pound for the area for that year, but apart from this there is no statutory ceiling, only the constraints imposed by the economic climate.

There is thus considerable scope for grant-aid in favour of a wide variety of voluntary organisations. This is particularly appropriate and mutually beneficial where non-statutory organisations operate in areas for which the authority has an overall statutory responsibility. For instance, a society for disabled people may provide holidays, aids, recreational facilities and voluntary services for its members, relieving to some extent claims upon the statutory services and the authority's obligations under the Chronically Sick and Disabled Persons Act 1970. In such circumstances, it seems right and proper that local authorities should help the voluntary sector: indeed, enlightened authorities would wish to encourage local voluntary endeavour, recognising that a relatively small expenditure can thereby go a long way and, conversely, realising the limitations, constraints and considerable expense which would be imposed upon them if they had to cope on a purely professional basis.

Normally, the local authority appoints a grants subcommittee for each of the committees having major powers to support voluntary organisations. The committees consider applications once a year and are advised by the officers of the authority working in the relevant fields and by the treasurer. They make their recommendations to a meeting of the whole council. The arrangements are thus less open to personal idiosyncracies and undue partiality than is sometimes the case with charitable trusts, but it is again probably fair to say that policy is likely to favour those who show a capacity for self-help.

From the applicant's point of view, timing is crucial. Estimates for the financial year which runs from 1 April to 31 March are prepared a long way in advance and much of the detailed work is done at least six months before the beginning of the financial year. Any organisation considering making an application for a grant for the first time should, therefore, aim to provide the local authority with all the relevant information *before 1 October* in relation to an application for the following financial year. Generally, organisations that have received a grant in the past will receive a reminder letter from the local authority that grants will be considered by a certain date and asking for appropriate information to be submitted.

Given the limited funds available, the application must be carefully and convincingly prepared and presented, and should be supported by the organisation's annual report and accounts. Sufficient copies should be provided to ensure that all concerned in taking the decision see *the original application*. There is no standard form of application, but the information suggested for submissions to charitable trusts (see page 139) will be equally relevant. It will help if it can also be shown that there are advantages to the local authority if the intended service is carried out on a voluntary basis, and that the proposed arrangements complement and do not overlap the authority's own provision. The authority is administering public money and will be particularly careful to ensure that grants are to be used effectively. It will wish to be absolutely satisfied that the organisation has sufficient management and financial expertise to support its programme and spend the money responsibly and wisely, and that there is a genuine and demonstrable need for the proposed activity.

Grants from central government and allied bodies

As local organisations can look to local authorities for help, so national organisations, working in a number of specialist fields, can seek assistance from central government. Each government department or specially appointed body acts independently under separate legislation, the principal benefactors being the Department of Health and Social Security, the Department of the Environment, the Arts Council and the Sports Council. A special section of the Home Office – the Voluntary Services Unit – will exceptionally deal with applications for aid where there is no relevant departmental source of funds or where the nature of the

143

project is within the ambit of more than one department.

Broadly speaking, central government, like local authorities, is most likely to support voluntary organisations where they are clearly providing services which complement or supplement statutory provision or, exceptionally, where they provide a preferable alternative to statutory services. It is beyond question that well run voluntary organisations can often provide services which at once are more personal and yield a better return for a given financial input than their professional counterparts. Far from diminishing since the development of the 'welfare state', the role of the voluntary sector has vastly increased in significance. The 1977 report of the Wolfenden Committee has underlined the vital and increasing contribution which voluntary organisations can make in the future, and there is every reason to hope and expect that governments, of whatever political colour, will give increasing financial encouragement to their efforts.

The basic rules for applications – simplicity and conciseness – apply here but perhaps more so. There may be a standard form of application. If not, keep to the *relevant* facts. If more detail is required it will be requested. Government departments must above all be satisfied that the proposals are in harmony with central government and departmental policy, and that the organisation making the application is of good repute and competent in every respect to carry through the project or service proposed. The financial year of central government is the same as that of local authorities, and it is therefore advisable to make application before 1 October for grants needed in the following financial year 1 April to 31 March. (An exception is grant-aid under the Urban Programme, where applications are specifically invited. See the next page.)

Grants from the Department of Education and Science

Two types of grant are considered:

1. Recurring assistance to help with the cost of the administrative expenses of national youth organisations whose objectives are broadly educational. Only properly constituted, voluntary, non-profit-making organisations having activities throughout the country may qualify. Such bodies will normally be registered as charities. They need not be *exclusively* concerned with young people, but grants are awarded in respect of services which are primarily for youth, roughly those aged 14 to 20.

Applications should be made to the Department of Education and Science, Higher and Further Education Branch 2, Elizabeth House, York Road, London SE1.

2. Capital grants for local educational projects. These are normally dependent upon prior support by local education authorities through whom applications must be channelled. However, capital projects which, although locally based, offer facilities on a national or regional basis are an exception to this rule and applications should be made direct to the Department. Examples are field study centres and conference centres.

Grants from the Department of the Environment

Aid is provided under the government's Urban Programme for the relief of social need in deprived urban areas. Typical are areas of low-quality environment, high unemployment, poverty and poor housing, but provision can also extend to areas where there is severe pressure on social services, e.g. because of exceptionally high proportions of old or disabled people, or where children are disadvantaged because of inadequate educational facilities.

Grants are payable only to local authorities, normally at a rate of 75 per cent of the total cost incurred, but the government encourages authorities to 'bear in mind the contribution which voluntary organisations can make to the relief of urban deprivation'. In practice, a significant proportion of the total aid is used to fund voluntary projects, and it is open to voluntary organisations to seek support from local authorities under the Urban Programme. The effect is that where a voluntary organisation is successful in obtaining a grant, one-quarter of the money is found by the local authority and the remainder by central government.

There are thus two hurdles to be overcome, and it would be unrealistic to suggest that it is easy to secure help under the Urban Programme. One must first win the support of the local authority, who must in turn press an application with the Department of the Environment. It will have to compete with other applications by the same authority and with those of other authorities for limited funds. At present, the demand for grants far exceeds the financial provision available in a given year. Nevertheless, applications for suitable projects should be pressed with vigour. If well presented so as to win the support and advocacy of the local authority they should stand a reasonable chance of success. In the financial year

1978/79 some £30 million is being made available for England and Wales and the government has announced that in the following year aid will be expanded to £125 million.

Timing is again crucial. The DOE issues regular circulars at approximately annual intervals, together with application forms (which are of some complexity), inviting applications from local authorities. Voluntary organisations seeking support under the Urban Programme need to ensure that they are kept informed of the receipt and terms of these circulars, and must be poised to present a reasoned and fully documented case at the appropriate time.

The seventeenth and latest circular (DOE 122/77) was issued on 30 November 1977 and invited applications for £10 million of new project funding. This was quickly followed by an announcement that further sums, amounting to over £15 million, would be made available to seven specified inner city areas. The DOE also invited grants for educational and recreational schemes for children and young people during the 1978 summer holidays. These were intended to help urban areas having a high level of social need and a scarcity of safe recreational facilities. More than 270 projects run by 74 local authorities were approved at a total cost of nearly £400,000. Voluntary organisations were involved in more than half of these schemes. Similar grants for Easter holiday projects costing £92,000 were also approved.

Urban Programme grants are made under the Local Government Grants (Social Need) Act 1969.

Grants from the Department of Health and Social Security

The Secretary of State for Social Services has powers under s. 64 of the Health Services and Public Health Act 1968 to give grants to voluntary organisations working in the health and personal social fields in the provision of services similar to those which it is the responsibility of the Secretary of State or a local authority to provide. Such grants are normally given to assist national organisations with the cost of providing a central back-up service to a national network.

In deciding whether, and to what extent, a voluntary organisation can be supported in this way, the DHSS normally takes into account the degree to which an organisation's activities will help to achieve the Department's broad policy objectives; whether the service provided is one that is regarded as being of particularly high priority, whether it represents a more effective use of its limited funds than the service provided by competing applicants for support; and the amount of money already available to the organisation from other sources for funding its activities.

Thus, when submitting applications for grant-aid, interested voluntary organisations who think they may be eligible, would be well advised to frame their submissions accordingly. They should give full details of their work, audited accounts where possible, and estimated totals of income and expenditure (including probable grants from other bodies) for the period and project for which they are seeking financial help.

Applications should be made to the Department of Health and Social Security, Alexander Fleming House, Elephant and Castle, London SE1 6BY.

Grants from the Manpower Services Commission

The Commission operates two special schemes aimed at alleviating some of the worst effects of the present high levels of unemployment. The Special Temporary Employment Programme (STEP) is intended to provide 25,000 temporary jobs in a full year for adults (19 and over) in projects similar to those previously mounted under the Job Creation Programme. The Youth Opportunities Programme (YOP) is for young people (16–18) and is intended to provide 234,000 places in a variety of training and work experience schemes.

Under both programmes, the Commission actively needs the co-operation of voluntary organisations to help to provide suitable opportunities. The primary condition is that the work offered should meet the needs of the unemployed person, not the other way round. The Youth Opportunities Programme clearly offers the greater scope. Voluntary organisations, along with local authorities, industry and commerce, can help by providing work experience opportunities in three areas – training workshops, special community projects and community service. The opportunities must be such as will provide an outlet for training and further education, allow the development of basic skills and meet the young people's individual needs.

By providing work experience on these terms, voluntary organisations at the same time help themselves. The young people employed receive a flat-rate weekly allowance of £19.50 while they are on the programme. This is paid by the organisation but reimbursed by the Commission. It is free of tax and national insurance contributions. In addition, the Commission will

147

contribute to the organisation's overheads – renting and re-furbishing premises, equipment, materials and supervision. The only thing the Commission cannot pay for is the outright purchase of land or buildings. Thus voluntary organisations are, as a by-product of their help to the programme, able to press ahead with desirable projects at low cost to themselves.

A booklet has been prepared by the Commission giving further information on the types of work experience programmes which are suitable. In general, proposals, as well as meeting the needs of unemployed young people, must be of benefit to the community and must not lead to private gain. Any voluntary organisation which thinks it might be able to help (and be helped) is advised to talk over its ideas with its nearest MSC Area Officer who will give all necessary guidance and an indication of whether an application is likely to succeed. Area offices are listed in the appendix at the back of the book.

Grants from the Arts Council of Great Britain

With government backing, the Arts Council provides financial assistance on a wide front for creative artists and for companies in the performing arts. It offers subsidies to drama, opera and dance companies, to orchestras, arts centres, and other relevant organisations in London and the regions. Grants can also be made in respect of particular productions, exhibitions or projects.

Almost all the arts-promoting organisations assisted by the Arts Council are established as non-profit-distributing bodies providing the arts as a service to the community. It is important to appreciate that such services are recognised as being charitable objects, and that as such an organisation providing them is likely to qualify for, and to be able to obtain the benefits of, registration as a charity with the Charity Commission.

A variety of award schemes are operated and vary between England, Scotland and Wales. Full details, the relevant conditions and application forms may be obtained from the following addresses, as appropriate:

Arts Council of Great Britain, 105 Piccadilly, London W1V 0AU; telephone 01 629 9495.

The Scottish Arts Council, 19 Charlotte Square, Edinburgh EH2 4DF; telephone 031 226 6051.

The Welsh Arts Council, Holst House, Museum Place, Cardiff CF1 3NX; telephone 0222 394711.

Regional Arts Associations

These combine at a regional level the work of the various national organisations such as the Arts Council, the British Film Institute and the Crafts Advisory Committee. They are independent and autonomous, being neither regional branches of the Arts Council, nor purely local authority associations, though they work in partnership with both.

Grant-aiding is a major function of most of the Regional Arts Associations, and the one to which the greatest part of their funds is allocated. They support, for example, orchestras and theatre companies, or the arts centres and societies which engage such companies. In certain cases, grants are made for projects or for specific items in larger events such as festivals. Both professional and amateur organisations are eligible for assistance, though in practice funds are mainly directed to professional activities, partly because their needs and expenses are greater, but more particularly because most amateur activities are seen as the responsibility of local rather than regional authorities. A list of RAAs will be supplied by the Arts Council on request.

Grants from the Sports Council

The Sports Council has 29 members appointed on behalf of the Secretary of State for the Environment by the Minister with responsibility for Sport and Recreation and is also grant-aided by the government (1977/78: £14.2 million). It is an independent body established by royal charter and decides its own policies on the promotion of sport.

The Council has a responsibility to allocate funds for the development of sport and recreation, and does so in the light of a careful and continuous review of new and developing sporting programmes as well as the need, from time to time, to give further impetus to established schemes.

Most of the grant-aid provided by the Council goes to the governing bodies of sport, to the capital and current costs of the national sports centres and facilities, and to local authorities towards the cost of capital projects. There is, however, some provision for voluntary clubs at local level. Almost invariably, voluntary organisations have to raise a part of the balance of cost of their projects by special fund-raising efforts. It is also a condition of grant that there should be evidence of financial need. Over the years 1972–1977, the Sports Council spent nearly £5 million on minor projects over a wide range of sports from angling to weightlifting. It has also encouraged local authorities to take responsibility under their statutory powers to support local club schemes and to promote the development of facilities and opportunities for sport as part of their community services. (In the financial years 1974/75 and 1975/76 the total grants offered by local authorities to local clubs were even greater than those offered by the Council.)

An area to which the Sports Council has given very special attention is that of sport and physical recreation for disabled people. The aim is clear: to promote, wherever possible, the integration of disabled people into community sport and to extend the range of activities in which they can participate enjoyably and safely. Grant-aid is offered to national bodies for administration, coaching, development, preparation training for international events and for travel costs of international teams going to approved events overseas. The Council recognises the British Sports Association for the Disabled as the coordinating and developing body for sport for the disabled, and offers substantial grant-aid to the Association as the umbrella body in this field. Total current grant-aid to sport for the disabled in 1976/77 amounted to £50,000.

The Council publishes the following useful free guides: *Capital Grants for Sports Facilities in Areas of Special Needs*, 1976; and *Capital Grants and Loans for Sports Facilities Promoted by Local Voluntary Organisations*, April 1977.

The Yorkshire and Humberside Regional Office (Coronet House, Queen Street, Leeds LS1 4PW) has published three guides under the title, *Grant Aid to Voluntary Sports Organisations*, price 50p each, covering the years 1968/73, 1972/75 and 1975/76.

The Sports Council headquarters are at 70 Brompton Road, London SW3 1EX; telephone 01 589 3411. There are nine regional offices whose addresses are listed in the appendix at the back of the book.

Voluntary Services Unit

The Voluntary Services Unit, based at the Home Office, has four main functions. First it is intended to act as a link between voluntary organisations and government departments, giving advice to the former about their best points of contact within departments and alerting the latter to the possible effects upon voluntary organisations of certain major policy proposals, legislation, or government directives. Secondly, it provides a useful focal point for the diverse departmental interests within Whitehall relating to the voluntary sector. For this purpose, the Unit has within each major government department a liaison officer who is responsible for keeping the Unit informed on matters relevant to its work and who attends quarterly meetings with the Unit and all the other liaison officers at which information and advice can be exchanged and matters of general interest to the voluntary sector can be discussed.

The third function of the Unit is to stimulate the use of volunteers where this can appropriately be done by central government and to encourage voluntary organisations to cooperate with each other and to coordinate their activities in an effort to avoid unnecessary duplication of effort. Finally, the Unit functions as a financier of last resort within Whitehall, with limited funds available to assist national organisations or projects whose work spans the interests of several different departments or which are not the direct responsibility of any single department. Its funds are also used in exceptional cases to support 'innovatory local projects from which lessons of national relevance can be learned', and to maintain organisations working in areas of high social priority where alternative funds will definitely be available within a short time.

The Voluntary Services Unit does not in any way interfere with the working relations already established between most government departments and the voluntary organisations concerned with the services for which those departments are responsible. Nor does it lead to any overall decisions about the optimum level of government expenditure on voluntary organisations. Each department decides, in relation to its priorities and resources, which organisation it will support and the extent to which such support will be given. The only general policy, which is a direct result of the current restraints on spending, is that departments should at present give priority to meeting existing commitments to voluntary organisations, should then assist, where possible, existing organisations whose work is of high social priority but likely to fail for lack of finance, and should then encourage new services or the extension of existing ones, again where the work is of high social priority.

Applications to the Unit may be made informally by letter. Advice can then be given on the most suitable basis and form of further action. The address of the Voluntary Services Unit is 50 Queen Anne's Gate, London SW1.

Other government aid

Other government aid includes:

1. Partial funding of organisations operating and financing development projects in the Third World. Grants to facilitate exchanges, visits and conferences for the benefit of developing countries. Further information from the Ministry of Overseas Development.

2. Financial support for organisations which provide employment, training, and rehabilitation services for disabled people. Further information from the Department of Employment.

3. Assistance with the costs of European and some Commonwealth visits and exchanges between non-governmental bodies. Further information from the Foreign and Commonwealth Office.

Appendix: useful addresses

Alexandra Rose Day
1 Castelnau, Barnes, London
SW13 9RP

Arts Councils:

Arts Council of Great Britain
105 Piccadilly, London
W1V 0AU (tel. 01 629 9495)

The Scottish Arts Council
19 Charlotte Square,
Edinburgh EH2 4DF (tel.
031 226 6051)

The Welsh Arts Council
Holst House, Museum Place,
Cardiff CF1 3NX (tel.
0222 394711)

Barnum's Carnival Novelties Ltd
67 Hammersmith Road, London
W14 8UY (tel. 01 602 1211)

British Broadcasting Corporation
The Appeals Secretary,
Broadcasting House, London
W1A 1AA

British Majorette Association
General Secretary, Mrs J.A.
Terry, 48 Brancaster Road,
Newbury Park, Ilford, Essex

Charities Aid Foundation
48 Pembury Road, Tonbridge,
Kent TN9 2JD (tel. 0732 356323)

Charity Commission
14 Ryder Street, London SW1

Chemical Recovery Association
Petrol House, Hepscott Road,
London E9 8HD

Civil Service Departments
(house-to-house collections) tel.
01 233 5404 – England
031 556 8400 – Scotland

Countryside Commission
John Dower House, Crescent
Place, Cheltenham,
Gloucestershire GL50 3RA

*Department of Education and
Science, Higher and Further
Education Branch 2*
Elizabeth House, York Road,
London SE1

*Department of Employment,
European Social Fund Division*
32 St. James's Square,
London SW1

*Department of the Environment,
Directorate of Information*
2 Marsham Street, London
SW1P 3EB

*Department of Health and Social
Security*
Alexander Fleming House,
Elephant and Castle, London
SE1 6BY

English Country Cheese Council
National Dairy Centre, John
Princes Street, London
W1M 0AP

153

*European Community Press and
Information Office*
20 Kensington Palace Gardens,
London W8 4QQ (tel.
01 727 8090)

Gaming Board
Africa House, 64/78 Kingsway,
London WC2B 6BW

*Glass Manufacturers Federation,
Recycling Bureau*
19 Portland Place, London
W1N 4BH

*Green Shield Trading Stamp
Company Ltd*
Green Shield House, Station
Road, Edgware, Middlesex
HA8 7AQ

*Independent Broadcasting
Authority*
The Appeals Secretary, 70
Brompton Road, London
SW3 1EY

*Inland Revenue, Claims Branch,
Charity Division*
Magdalen House, Trinity Road,
Bootle, Merseyside L69 9BB

Local Radio Stations (BBC):

BBC Radio Birmingham
Pebble Mill Road,
Birmingham B5 7SA (tel.
021 472 5141; telex 339210)

BBC Radio Blackburn
King Street, Blackburn, Lancs
BB2 2EA (tel. 0254 62411;
telex 63491)

BBC Radio Brighton
Marlborough Place, Brighton,
East Sussex BN1 1TU (tel.
0273 680231; telex 87313)

BBC Radio Bristol
3 Tyndalls Park Road, Bristol
BS8 1PP (tel. 0272 311111;
telex 449170)

BBC Radio Carlisle
Hilltop Heights, London
Road, Carlisle, Cumbria
CA1 2NA (tel. 0228 31661;
telex 64165)

BBC Radio Cleveland
PO Box 194, 91/3 Linthorpe
Road, Middlesbrough,
Cleveland TS1 5DG (tel.
0642 248491; telex 58203)

BBC Radio Derby
56 St. Helen's Street, Derby
DE1 3HY (tel. 0332 361111;
telex 37257)

BBC Radio Humberside
9 Chapel Street, Hull, North
Humberside HU1 3NU (tel.
0482 23232; telex 527031)

BBC Radio Leeds
Broadcasting House,
Woodhouse Lane, Leeds
LS2 9PN (tel. 0532 42131;
telex 57230)

BBC Radio Leicester
Epic House, Charles Street,
Leicester LE1 3SH (tel.
0533 27113; telex 34401)

BBC Radio London
PO Box 4LG, 35a Marylebone
High Street, London
W1A 4LG (tel. 01 486 7611;
telex 267223)

BBC Radio Manchester
PO Box 90, New Broadcasting
House, Oxford Road,
Manchester M60 1SJ (tel.
061 228 3434; telex 668708)

BBC Radio Medway
30 High Street, Chatham, Kent
ME4 4EZ (tel. 0634 46284;
telex 965011)

BBC Radio Merseyside
Commerce House, 13/17 Sir
Thomas Street, Liverpool
L1 5BS (tel. 051 236 3355;
telex 62364)

BBC Radio Newcastle
Crestina House, Archbold
Terrace, Newcastle upon Tyne
NE2 1DZ (tel. 0632 814243;
telex 537007)

BBC Radio Nottingham
York House, York Street,
Nottingham NG1 3JB (tel.
0602 47643; telex 37464)

BBC Radio Oxford
242/254 Banbury Road,
Oxford OX2 7DW (tel.
0865 53411; telex 83571)

BBC Radio Sheffield
Ashdell Grove, 60 Westbourne
Road, Sheffield S10 2QU (tel.
0742 686185; telex 54400)

BBC Radio Solent
South Western House, Canute
Road, Southampton SO9 4PJ
(tel. 0703 31311; telex 47420)

BBC Radio Stoke-on-Trent
Conway House, Cheapside,
Hanley, Stoke-on-Trent, Staffs
ST1 1JJ (tel. 0782 24827; telex
36104)

*For further information
contact*
The Local Radio Publicity
Officer, Room 227, The
Langham, Portland Place,
London W1 (tel. 01 580 4468
ex 2887/3647)

*Local Radio Stations
(Independent Broadcasting
Authority):*

Beacon Radio 303
267 Tettenhall Road,
Wolverhampton, West
Midlands WV6 0DQ (tel.
0902 757211)

BRMB Radio
Radio House, Aston Road
North, Birmingham B6 4BX
(tel. 021 359 4481)

Capital Radio
Euston Tower, London
NW1 3DR (tel. 01 388 1288)

Downtown Radio
Kiltonga Radio Centre, PO
Box 293, Newtownards, Co.
Down (tel. 0247 815555)

LBC
Communications House,
Gough Square, Fleet Street,
London EC4P 4LP (tel.
01 353 1010)

Metro Radio
Radio House, Longrigg,
Swalwell, Newcastle upon
Tyne NE99 1BB (tel.
0632 884121)

Pennine Radio
Pennine House, Forster
Square, Bradford, West
Yorkshire BD1 5NP (tel.
0274 31521)

Piccadilly Radio
127/131 The Piazza, Piccadilly
Plaza, Manchester M1 4AW
(tel. 061 236 9913)

Plymouth Sound
Earl's Acre, Alma Road,
Plymouth, Devon PL3 4HL
(tel. 0752 27272)

Radio City
PO Box 194, Liverpool
L69 1LD (tel. 051 227 5100)

Radio Clyde
Ranken House, Blythswood
Court, Anderston Cross
Centre, Glasgow G2 7LB (tel.
041 204 2555)

Radio Forth
Forth House, Forth Street,
Edinburgh EH1 3LF (tel.
031 556 9255)

Radio Hallam
PO Box 194, Hartshead,
Sheffield S1 1GP (tel.
0742 71188)

Radio Orwell
Electric House, Lloyds
Avenue, Ipswich, Suffolk
IP1 3HU (tel. 0473 216971)

Radio Tees
74 Dovecot Street, Stockton-
on-Tees, Cleveland TS18 1LL
(tel. 0642 615111)

Radio Trent
29/31 Castle Gate,
Nottingham NG1 7AT (tel.
0602 581732)

Radio Victory
PO Box 257, Portsmouth,
Hants PO1 5RT (tel.
0705 27799)

Swansea Sound
Victoria Road, Gowerton,
Swansea, West Glam SA4 3AB
(tel. 0792 893751)

Thames Valley Broadcasting
PO Box 210, Reading,
Berkshire RG3 5RZ (tel.
0734 413151)

*Manpower Services Commission
(* denotes temporary
arrangement):*

Birmingham*
George House, George Road,
Five Ways, Edgbaston,
Birmingham (tel. 021 454 2995)

Bristol
The Pithay, Bristol BS1 1NQ
(tel. 0272 291071)

Cardiff*
4th Floor, Phase One
Building, Tyglas, Llanishen,
Cardiff CF4 5PJ (tel.
0222 762641)

Carlisle Sub-office*
1 Victoria Place, Carlisle,
Cumbria CA1 1HG (tel.
0228 39411)
Coventry*
5th Floor, Bankfield House,
New Union Street, Coventry,
West Midlands CV1 2PE (tel.
0203 56561)

Dumfries
139 Irish Street, Dumfries (tel.
0387 5161)

Dundee*
5 Whitehall Crescent, Dundee
(tel. 0382 22575)

Edinburgh
Meldrum House, Drumsheugh
Gardens, Edinburgh EH3 7QG
(tel. 031 225 1313)

Exeter
Central Station Chambers,
Queen Street, Exeter EX4 3RZ
(tel. 0392 38711)

Glasgow*
440 Sauchiehall Street,
Glasgow G2 3JX (tel.
041 332 9722)

High Wycombe*
19a Crendon Street, High
Wycombe, Bucks (tel.
0494 41518)

Horsham
TSA District Office, Exchange
House, Worthing Road,
Horsham, West Sussex (tel.
0403 50342)

Hull
Government Buildings, Spring
Bank, Hull, North
Humberside HU3 1LR (tel.
0482 226491)

Inverness Sub-office*
42a Union Street, Inverness
(tel. 0463 39361)

Ipswich
Haven House, 17 Lower
Brook Street, Ipswich, Suffolk
(tel. 0473 212388)

Leeds
Pennine House, Russell Street,
Leeds LS1 5RN (tel.
0532 41417)

Liverpool
2nd Floor, 27 Leece Street,
Liverpool L1 2TS (tel.
051 708 7357)

London
Hanway House, 27 Red Lion
Square, London WC1 (tel.
01 405 8454)

Manchester
First Floor, 14/22 The
Parsonage, Alexandra House,
Manchester M3 2JA (tel.
061 833 0413 and 0581)

Middlesbrough*
The Skill Centre, Queensway,
Middlesbrough, Cleveland
TS3 8JQ (tel. 0642 219336)

Nottingham*
3rd Floor, Cranbrook House,
Cranbrook Street, Nottingham
NG1 1ES (tel. 0602 46121)

Sheffield*
The Job Centre, Firth Park
Road, Firth Park, Sheffield
(tel. 0742 611331)

Southampton
TSA District Office, Queen's
Park House, 2/8 Queen's
Terrace, Southampton
SQ1 1BP (tel. 0703 29636 and
29872)

Sunderland
38 Market Square,
Sunderland, Tyne and Wear
TS1 3LP (tel. 0783 43316)

Swansea
2nd Floor, Orchard House,
Orchard Street, Swansea, West
Glamorgan (tel. 0792 462652)

Wolverhampton*
TSA District Office, 2nd
Floor, Pearl Assurance House,
15/17 Waterloo Road,
Wolverhampton, West
Midlands, WV1 4BU (tel.
0902 771704)

Wrexham*
TSA District Office, 2nd
Floor, 1/2 Imperial Building,
King Street, Wrexham, Clwyd
LL11 1NR (tel. 0978 55606)

Materials Reclamation Weekly
PO Box NG 109, Davis House,
66/77 High Street, Croydon,
Surrey CR9 1QH

National Anti-Waste Programme
Ashdown House, 123 Victoria
Street, London SW1E 6RB

*National Council of Social
Service*
24 Bedford Square, London
WC1B 3HU

*National Milk Publicity Council
Inc*
c/o W.E. Tucker Ltd,
Twinstead, Sudbury, Suffolk

Oxfam Wastesaver
274 Banbury Road, Oxford
OX2 7DZ (tel. 0865 56777)

*Royal Society for the Prevention
of Accidents*
Cannon House, The Priory
Queensway, Birmingham B4 6BS

*Spastics Society Waste
Reclamation Depot*
16 Bridge Road East, Welwyn
Garden City, Hertfordshire

Sports Council
70 Brompton Road, London
SW3 1EX (tel. 01 589 3411)

Regional Offices:
Eastern Region
26/8 Bromham Road, Bedford
MK40 2QD

East Midlands Region
26 Musters Road, West
Bridgford, Nottingham
NG2 7PL

*Greater London and South
East Region*
160 Great Portland Street,
London W1N 5TB

Northern Region
County Court Building,
Hallgarth Street, Durham
DH1 3PB

North West Region
Byrom House, Quay Street,
Manchester M3 5FJ

Southern Region
Watlington House,
Watlington Street, Reading,
Berkshire RG1 4RJ

South Western Region
Ashlands House, Ashlands,
Crewkerne, Somerset
TA18 7LQ

West Midlands Region
Crest House, 7 Highfield
Road, Edgbaston,
Birmingham B15 3EG

*Yorkshire and Humberside
Region*
Coronet House, Queen Street,
Leeds LS1 4PW

UK Press Gazette
Cliffords Inn, Fetter Lane,
London EC4A 1PJ

Voluntary Services Unit
50 Queen Anne's Gate,
London SW1

Young Volunteer Force
60 Highbury Grove, London N5
(tel. 01 226 5375)

Index